THE COMPLETE TESTIMONY OF THE FATHERS OF THE FIRST THREE CENTURIES CONCERNING THE SABBATH AND FIRST DAY

LECTOR HOUSE PUBLIC DOMAIN WORKS

THE COMPLETE TESTIMONY OF THE FATHERS OF THE FIRST THREE CENTURIES CONCERNING THE SABBATH AND FIRST DAY

JOHN NEVINS ANDREWS

ISBN: 978-93-5614-012-7

Published: 1876

LECTOR HOUSE LLP
E-MAIL: lectorpublishing@gmail.com

THE COMPLETE TESTIMONY OF THE FATHERS OF THE FIRST THREE CENTURIES CONCERNING THE SABBATH AND FIRST DAY

BY

ELD. J. N. ANDREWS

SECOND EDITION.

1876.

PREFACE.

The testimony for first-day sacredness is very meager in the Scriptures, as even its own advocates must admit. But they have been wont to supply the deficiency by a plentiful array of testimonies from the early fathers of the church. Here, in time past, they have had the field all to themselves, and they have allowed their zeal for the change of the Sabbath to get the better of their honesty and their truthfulness. The first-day Sabbath was absolutely unknown before the time of Constantine. Nearly one hundred years elapsed after John was in vision on Patmos before the term "Lord's day" was applied to the first day. During this time, it was called "the day of the sun," "the first day of the week," and "the eighth day." The first writers who gave it the name of "Lord's day," state the remarkable fact that in their judgement the true Lord's day consists of every day of a Christian's life, a very convincing proof that they did not give this title to Sunday because John had so named it on Patmos. In fact, no one of those who give this title to Sunday ever assigned as a reason for so doing that it was thus called by John. Nor is there any intimation in one of the fathers that first-day observance was an act of obedience to the fourth commandment, nor one clear statement that ordinary labor on that day was sinful. In order to show these facts, I have undertaken to give every testimony of every one of the fathers, prior to A. D. 325, who mentions either the Sabbath or the first day. Though some of these quotations are comparatively unimportant, others are of very great value. I have given them all, in order that the reader may actually possess their entire testimony. I have principally followed the translation of the "Ante-Nicene Christian Library," and have in every case made use of first-day translations. The work has been one of great labor to me, and I trust will be found of much profit to the candid reader.

J. N. ANDREWS.

Lancaster, Mass., Jan. 1, 1873.

PREFACE TO THE SECOND EDITION.

In this edition every quotation has been carefully compared with the works of the fathers from which they were taken. A few minor errors have been detected, but none of importance. The work is commended to the attention of candid inquirers with the prayer that God will make it instrumental in opening the eyes of many to the truth concerning his holy day.

J. N. A.

Neuchâtel, Switzerland, April 7, 1876.

CONTENTS

TESTIMONY OF THE FATHERS.

CHAPTER I.

INTRODUCTORY STATEMENT.

With respect to the Sabbath, the religious world may be divided into three classes:—

1. Those who retain the ancient seventh-day Sabbath.

2. Those who observe the first-day Sabbath.

3. Those who deny the existence of any Sabbath.[1]

It is inevitable that controversy should exist between these parties. Their first appeal is to the Bible, and this should decide the case; for it reveals man's whole duty. But there is an appeal by the second party, and sometimes by the third, to another authority, the early fathers of the church, for the decision of the question.

The controversy stands thus: The second and third parties agree with the first that God did anciently require the observance of the seventh day; but both deny the doctrine of the first, that he still requires men to hallow that day; the second asserting that he has changed the Sabbath to the first day of the week; and the third declaring that he has totally abolished the institution itself.

The first class plant themselves upon the plain letter of the law of God, and adduce those scriptures which teach the perpetuity and immutability of the moral law, and which show that the new covenant does not abrogate that law, but puts it into the heart of every Christian.

The second class attempt to prove the change of the Sabbath by quoting those texts which mention the first day of the week, and also those which are said to refer to it. The first day is, on such authority, called by this party the Christian Sabbath, and the fourth commandment is used by them to enforce this new Sabbath.

The third class adduce those texts which assert the dissolution of the old covenant; and those which teach the abolition of the ceremonial law with all its distinction of days, as new moons, feast days, and annual sabbaths; and also those texts

---

[1] Those who compose this class are unanimous in the view that the Sunday festival was established by the church; and they all agree in making it their day of worship, but not for the same reason; for, while one part of them devoutly accept the institution as the Lord's day on the authority of the church, the other part make it their day for worship simply because it is the most convenient day.

which declare that men cannot be justified by that law which condemns sin; and from all these contend that the law and the Sabbath are both abolished.

But the first class answer to the second that the texts which they bring forward do not meet the case, inasmuch as they say nothing respecting the change of the Sabbath; and that it is not honest to use the fourth commandment to enforce the observance of a day not therein commanded. And the third class assent to this answer as truthful and just.

To the position of the third class, the first make this answer: That the old covenant was made between God and his people *concerning* his law;[2] that it ceased because the people failed in its conditions, the keeping of the commandments; that the new covenant does not abrogate the law of God, but secures obedience to it by putting it into the heart of every Christian; that there are two systems of law, one being made up of typical and ceremonial precepts, and the other consisting of moral principles only; that those texts which speak of the abrogation of the handwriting of ordinances and of the distinction in meats, drinks, and days, pertain alone to this shadowy system, and never to the moral law which contains the Sabbath of the Lord; and that it is not the fault of the law, but of sinners, that they are condemned by it; and that justification being attained only by the sacrifice of Christ as a sin offering, is in itself a most powerful attestation to the perpetuity, immutability, and perfection, of that law which reveals sin. And to this answer the second class heartily assent.

But the second class have something further to say. The Bible, indeed, fails to assert the change of the Sabbath, but these persons have something else to offer, in their estimation, equally as good as the Scriptures. The early fathers of the church, who conversed with the apostles, or who conversed with some who had conversed with them, and those who followed for several generations, are by this class presented as authority, and their testimony is used to establish the so-called Christian Sabbath on a firm basis. And this is what they assert respecting the fathers: That they distinctly teach the change of the Sabbath from the seventh to the first day of the week, and that the first day is by divine authority the Christian Sabbath.

But the third class squarely deny this statement, and affirm that the fathers held the Sabbath as an institution made for the Jews when they came out of Egypt, and that Christ abolished it at his death. They also assert that the fathers held the first day, not as a Sabbath in which men must not labor lest they break a divine precept, but as an ecclesiastical institution, which they called the Lord's day, and which was the proper day for religious assemblies because custom and tradition thus concurred. And so the third class answer the second by an explicit denial of its alleged facts. They also aim a blow at the first by the assertion that the early fathers taught the no-Sabbath doctrine, which must therefore be acknowledged as the real doctrine of the New Testament.

And now the first class respond to these conflicting statements of the second and the third. And here is their response:—

[2] Such is the exact nature of the covenant mentioned in Ex. 24:8; and Paul, in Heb. 9:18-20, quotes this passage, calling the covenant therein mentioned "the first testament," or covenant.

1. That our duty respecting the Sabbath, and respecting every other thing, can be learned only from the Scriptures.

2. That the first three hundred years after the apostles nearly accomplished the complete development of the great apostasy, which had commenced even in Paul's time; and this age of apostatizing cannot be good authority for making changes in the law of God.

3. That only a small proportion of the ministers and teachers of this period have transmitted any writings to our time; and these are generally fragments of the original works, and they have come down to us mainly through the hands of the Romanists, who have never scrupled to destroy or to corrupt that which witnesses against themselves, whenever it has been in their power to do it.

4. But inasmuch as these two classes, viz., those who maintain the first-day Sabbath, and those who deny the existence of any Sabbath, both appeal to these fathers for testimony with which to sustain themselves, and to put down the first class, viz., those who hallow the ancient Sabbath, it becomes necessary that the exact truth respecting the writings of that age, which now exist, should be shown. There is but one method of doing this which will effectually end the controversy. This is to give every one of their testimonies concerning the Sabbath and first-day in their own words. In doing this the following facts will appear:—

1. That in some important particulars there is a marked disagreement on this subject among them. For while some teach that the Sabbath originated at creation and should be hallowed even now, others assert that it began with the fall of the manna, and ended with the death of Christ. And while one class represent Christ as a violator of the Sabbath, another class represent him as sacredly hallowing it, and a third class declare that he certainly did violate it, and that he certainly never did, but always observed it! Some of them also affirm that the Sabbath was abolished, and in other places positively affirm that it is perpetuated and made more sacred than it formerly was. Moreover, some assert that the ten commandments are absolutely abolished, whilst others declare that they are perpetuated, and are the tests of Christian character in this dispensation. Some call the day of Christ's resurrection the first day of the week; others call it the day of the sun, and the eighth day; and a larger number call it the Lord's day, but there are no examples of this application till the close of the second century. Some enjoin the observance of both the Sabbath and the first day, while others treat the seventh day as despicable.

2. But in several things of great importance there is perfect unity of sentiment. They always distinguish between the Sabbath and the first day of the week. The change of the Sabbath from the seventh day to the first is never mentioned in a single instance. They never term the first day the Christian Sabbath, nor do they treat it as a Sabbath of any kind. Nor is there a single declaration in any of them that labor on the first day of the week is sinful; the utmost that can be found being one or two vague expressions which do not necessarily have any such sense.

3. Many of the fathers call the first day of the week the Lord's day. But none of them claim for it any scriptural authority, and some expressly state that it has none

whatever, but rests solely upon custom and tradition.

4. But the writings of the fathers furnish positive proof that the Sabbath was observed in the Christian church down to the time when they wrote, and by no inconsiderable part of that body. For some of them expressly enjoined its observance, and even some of those who held that it was abolished speak of Christians who observed it, whom they would consent to fellowship if they would not make it a test.

5. And now mark the work of apostasy: This work never begins by thrusting out God's institutions, but always by bringing in those of men and at first only asking that they may be tolerated, while yet the ones ordained of God are sacredly observed. This, in time, being effected, the next effort is to make them equal with the divine. When this has been accomplished, the third stage of the process is to honor them above those divinely commanded; and this is speedily succeeded by the fourth, in which the divine institution is thrust out with contempt, and the whole ground given to its human rival.

6. Before the first three centuries had expired, apostasy concerning the Sabbath had, with many of the fathers, advanced to the third stage, and with a considerable number had already entered upon the fourth. For those fathers who hallow the Sabbath do generally associate with it the festival called by them the Lord's day. And though they speak of the Sabbath as a divine institution, and never speak thus of the so-called Lord's day, they do, nevertheless, give the greater honor to this human festival. So far had the apostasy progressed before the end of the third century, that only one thing more was needed to accomplish the work as far as the Sabbath was concerned, and this was to discard it, and to honor the Sunday festival alone. Some of the fathers had already gone thus far; and the work became general within five centuries after Christ.

7. The modern church historians make very conflicting statements respecting the Sabbath during the first centuries. Some pass over it almost in silence, or indicate that it was, at most, observed only by Jewish Christians. Others, however, testify to its general observance by the Gentile Christians; yet some of these assert that the Sabbath was observed as a matter of expediency and not of moral obligation, because those who kept it did not believe the commandments were binding. (This is a great error, as will appear in due time.) What is said, however, by these modern historians is comparatively unimportant inasmuch as their sources of information were of necessity the very writings which are about to be quoted.

8. In the following pages will be found, in their own words, every statement[3] which the fathers of the first three centuries make by way of defining their views of the Sabbath and first-day. And even when they merely allude to either day in giving their views of other subjects, the nature of the allusion is stated, and, where practicable, the sentence or phrase containing it is quoted. The different writings are cited in the order in which they purport to have been written. A considerable number were not written by the persons to whom they were ascribed, but at a

[3] The case of Origen is a partial exception. Not all his works have been accessible to the writer, but sufficient of them have been examined to lay before the reader a just representation of his doctrine.

later date. As these have been largely quoted by first-day writers, they are here given in full. And even these writings possess a certain historical value. For though not written by the ones whose names they bear, they are known to have been in existence since the second or third century, and they give some idea of the views which then prevailed.

First of all let us hear the so-called "Apostolical Constitutions." These were not the work of the apostles, but they were in existence as early as the third century, and were then very generally believed to express the doctrine of the apostles. They do therefore furnish important historical testimony to the practice of the church at that time. Mosheim in his Historical Commentaries, Cent. 1, sect. 51, speaks thus of these "Constitutions": —

> "The matter of this work is unquestionably ancient; since the manners and discipline of which it exhibits a view are those which prevailed amongst the Christians of the second and third centuries, especially those resident in Greece and the oriental regions."

Of the "Apostolical Constitutions," Guericke's Church History speaks thus: —

> "This is a collection of ecclesiastical statutes purporting to be the work of the apostolic age, but in reality formed gradually in the second, third, and fourth centuries, and is of much value in reference to the history of polity, and Christian archæology generally." — *Ancient Church*, p. 212.

CHAPTER II.
TESTIMONY OF THE APOSTOLICAL CONSTITUTIONS.

"Have before thine eyes the fear of God, and always remember the ten commandments of God,—to love the one and only Lord God with all thy strength; to give no heed to idols, or any other beings, as being lifeless gods, or irrational beings or dæmons. Consider the manifold workmanship of God, which received its beginning through Christ. Thou shalt observe the Sabbath, on account of Him who ceased from his work of creation, but ceased not from his work of providence: it is a rest for meditation of the law, not for idleness of the hands." Book ii., sect. 4, par. 36.

This is sound Sabbatarian doctrine. But apostasy had begun its work in the establishment of the so-called Lord's day, which was destined in time to drive out the Sabbath. The next mention of the Sabbath also introduces the festival called Lord's day, but the reader will remember that this was written, not in the first century, but the third:—

"Let your judicatures be held on the second day of the week, that if any controversy arise about your sentence, having an interval till the Sabbath, you may be able to set the controversy right, and to reduce those to peace who have the contests one with another against the Lord's day." Book ii., sect. 6, par. 47.

By the term Lord's day the first day of the week is here intended. But the writer does not call the first day the Sabbath, that term being applied to the seventh day.

In section 7, paragraph 59, Christians are commanded to assemble for worship "every day, morning and evening, singing psalms and praying in the Lord's house: in the morning saying the sixty-second psalm, and in the evening the hundred and fortieth, but principally on the Sabbath day. And on the day of our Lord's resurrection, which is the Lord's day, meet more diligently, sending praise to God that made the universe by Jesus and sent him to us." "Otherwise what apology will he make to God who does not assemble on that day to hear the saving word concerning the resurrection, on which we pray thrice standing, in memory of him who arose in three days, in which is performed the reading of the prophets, the preaching of the gospel, the oblation of the sacrifice, the gift of the holy food."

The writer of these "Constitutions" this time gives the first day great prominence, though still honoring the Sabbath, and by no means giving that title to Sunday. But in book v., section 2, paragraph 10, we have a singular testimony to the manner in which Sunday was spent. Thus the writer says:—

> "Now we exhort you, brethren and fellow-servants, to avoid vain talk and obscene discourses, and jestings, drunkenness, lasciviousness, luxury, unbounded passions, with foolish discourses, since we do not permit you so much as on the Lord's days, which are days of joy, to speak or act anything unseemly."

From this it appears that the so-called Lord's day was a day of greater mirth than the other days of the week. In book v., section 3, paragraph 14, it is said:—

> "But when the first day of the week dawned he arose from the dead, and fulfilled those things which before his passion he foretold to us, saying: 'The Son of man must continue in the heart of the earth three days and three nights.'"

In book v., section 3, paragraph 15, the writer names the days on which Christians should fast:—

> "But he commanded us to fast on the fourth and sixth days of the week; the former on account of his being betrayed, and the latter on account of his passion. But he appointed us to break our fast on the seventh day at the cock-crowing, but to fast on the Sabbath day. Not that the Sabbath day is a day of fasting, being the rest from the creation, but because we ought to fast on this one Sabbath only, while on this day the Creator was under the earth."

In paragraph 17, Christians are forbidden to "celebrate the day of the resurrection of our Lord on any other day than a Sunday." In paragraph 18, they are again charged to fast on that one Sabbath which comes in connection with the anniversary of our Lord's death. In paragraph 19, the first day of the week is four times called the Lord's day. The period of 40 days from his resurrection to his ascension is to be observed. The anniversary of Christ's resurrection is to be celebrated by the supper.

> "And let this be an everlasting ordinance till the consummation of the world, until the Lord come. For to Jews the Lord is still dead, but to Christians he is risen: to the former, by their unbelief; to the latter, by their full assurance of faith. For the hope in him is immortal and eternal life. After eight days let there be another feast observed with honor, the eighth day itself, on which he gave me, Thomas, who was hard of belief, full assurance, by showing me the print of the nails, and the wound made in his side by the spear. And again, from the first Lord's day count forty days, from the Lord's day till the fifth day of the week, and celebrate the feast of the ascension of the Lord, whereon he finished all his dispensa-

tion and constitution," etc.

The things here commanded can come only once in a year. These are the anniversary of Christ's resurrection, and of that day on which he appeared to Thomas, and these were to be celebrated by the supper. The people were also to observe the day of the ascension on the fifth day of the week, forty days from his resurrection, on which day he finished his work. In paragraph 20, they are commanded to celebrate the anniversary of the Pentecost.

> "But after ten days from the ascension, which from the first Lord's day is the fiftieth day, do ye keep a great festival; for on that day, at the third hour, the Lord Jesus sent on us the gift of the Holy Ghost."

This was not a weekly but a yearly festival. Fasting is also set forth in this paragraph, but every Sabbath except the one Christ lay in the tomb is exempted from this fast, and every so-called Lord's day: —

> "We enjoin you to fast every fourth day of the week, and every day of the preparation [the sixth day], and the surplusage of your fast bestow upon the needy; every Sabbath day excepting one, and every Lord's day, hold your solemn assemblies, and rejoice; for he will be guilty of sin who fasts on the Lord's day, being the day of the resurrection, or during the time of Pentecost, or, in general, who is sad on a festival day to the Lord. For on them we ought to rejoice, and not to mourn."

This writer asserts that it is a sin to fast or mourn on Sunday, but never intimates that it is a sin to labor on that day when not engaged in worship. We shall next learn that the decalogue is in agreement with the law of nature, and that it is of perpetual obligation: —

> In book vi., section 4, paragraph 19, it is said: "He gave a plain law to assist the law of nature, such an one as is pure, saving, and holy, in which his own name was inscribed, perfect, which is never to fail, being complete in ten commands, unspotted, converting souls."

> In paragraph 20 it is said: "Now the law is the decalogue, which the Lord promulgated to them with an audible voice."

> In paragraph 22 he says: "You therefore are blessed who are delivered from the curse. For Christ, the Son of God, by his coming has confirmed and completed the law, but has taken away the additional precepts, although not all of them, yet at least the more grievous ones; having confirmed the former, and abolished the latter." And he further testifies as follows: "And besides, before his coming he refused the sacrifices of the people, while they frequently offered them, when they sinned against him, and thought he was to be appeased by sacrifices, but not by repentance."

For this reason the writer truthfully testifies that God refused to accept their burnt-offerings and sacrifices, their new moons and their Sabbaths.

In book vi., section 23, he says: "He who had commanded to honor our parents, was himself subject to them. He who had commanded to keep the Sabbath, by resting thereon for the sake of meditating on the laws, has now commanded us to consider of the law of creation, and of providence every day, and to return thanks to God."

This savors somewhat of the doctrine that all days are alike. Yet this cannot be the meaning; for in book vii., section 2, paragraph 23, he enjoins the observance of the Sabbath, and also of the Lord's-day festival, but specifies one Sabbath in the year in which men should fast. Thus he says:—

"But keep the Sabbath, and the Lord's-day festival; because the former is the memorial of the creation, and the latter, of the resurrection. But there is one only Sabbath to be observed by you in the whole year, which is that of our Lord's burial, on which men ought to keep a fast, but not a festival. For inasmuch as the Creator was then under the earth, the sorrow for him is more forcible than the joy for the creation; for the Creator is more honorable by nature and dignity than his own creatures."

In book vii., section 2, paragraph 30, he says: "On the day of the resurrection of the Lord, that is, the Lord's day, assemble yourselves together, without fail, giving thanks to God," etc.

In paragraph 36, the writer brings in the Sabbath again: "O Lord Almighty, thou hast created the world by Christ, and hast appointed the Sabbath in memory thereof, because that on *that day* thou hast made us *rest from our works*, for the meditation upon thy laws."

In the same paragraph, in speaking of the resurrection of Christ, the writer says:—

"On which account we solemnly assemble to celebrate the feast of the resurrection on the Lord's day," etc. In the same paragraph he speaks again of the Sabbath: "Thou didst give them the law or decalogue, which was pronounced by thy voice and written with thy hand. Thou didst enjoin the observation of the Sabbath, not affording them an occasion of idleness, but an opportunity of piety, for their knowledge of thy power, and the prohibition of evils; having limited them as within an holy circuit for the sake of doctrine, for the rejoicing upon the seventh period."

In this paragraph he also states his views of the Sabbath, and of the day which he calls the Lord's day, giving the precedence to the latter:—

"On this account he permitted men every Sabbath to rest, that so no one might be willing to send one word out of his mouth in anger on the day of the Sabbath. For the Sabbath is the ceasing of the creation, the completion of the world, the inquiry after laws, and the grateful praise to God for the blessings he has bestowed upon men. All which the Lord's day excels, and shows the Mediator himself, the Provider, the Law-giver, the Cause of the resurrection, the First-born of the whole creation," etc. And he adds: "So that the Lord's day commands us to offer unto thee, O Lord, thanksgiving for all. For this is the grace afforded by thee, which on account of its greatness has obscured all other blessings."

It is certainly noteworthy that the so-called Lord's day, for which no divine warrant is produced, is here exalted above the Sabbath of the Lord notwithstanding the Sabbath is acknowledged to be the divine memorial of the creation, and to be expressly enjoined in the decalogue, which the writer declares to be of perpetual obligation. Tested by his own principles, he had far advanced in apostasy; for he held a human festival more honorable than one which he acknowledged to be ordained of God; and only a single step remained; viz., to set aside the commandment of God for the ordinance of man.

In book viii., section 2, paragraph 4, it is said, when a bishop has been chosen and is to be ordained, —

> "Let the people assemble, with the presbytery and bishops that are present, on the Lord's day, and let them give their consent."

In book viii., section 4, paragraph 33, occurs the final mention of these two days in the so-called "Apostolical Constitutions."

> "Let the slaves work five days; but on the Sabbath day and the Lord's day let them have leisure to go to church for instruction in piety. We have said that the Sabbath is on account of the creation, and the Lord's day, of the resurrection."

To this may be added the 64th Canon of the Apostles, which is appended to the "Constitutions": —

> "If any one of the clergy be found to fast on the Lord's day, or on the Sabbath day, excepting one only, let him be deprived; but if he be one of the laity, let him be suspended."

Every mention of the Sabbath and first-day in that ancient book called "Apostolical Constitutions" is now before the reader. This book comes down to us from the third century, and contains what was at that time very generally believed to be the doctrine of the apostles. It is therefore valuable to us, not as authority respecting the teaching of the apostles, but as giving us a knowledge of the views and practices which prevailed in the third century. At the time these "Constitutions" were put in writing, the ten commandments were revered as the immutable rule of right, and the Sabbath of the Lord was by many observed as an act of obedience to the fourth commandment, and as the divine memorial of the creation. But the first-day festival had already attained such strength and influence as to clearly indicate that ere long it would claim the entire ground. But observe that the Sabbath and the so-called Lord's day are treated as distinct institutions, and that no hint of the change of the Sabbath to the first day of the week is ever once given. The "Apostolical Constitutions" are cited first, not because written by the apostles, but because of their title. For the same reason the so-called Epistle of Barnabas is quoted next, not because written by that apostle, for the proof is ample that it was not, but because it is often quoted by first-day writers as the words of the apostle Barnabas. It was in existence, however, as early as the middle of the second century, and, like the "Apostolical Constitutions," is of value to us in that it gives some clue to the opinions which prevailed in the region where the writer lived, or at least which were held by his party.

CHAPTER III.

Barnabas—Pliny—Ignatius—The Church at Smyrna—The Epistle to Diognetus—Recognitions of Clement—Syriac Documents concerning Edessa.

TESTIMONY OF THE EPISTLE OF BARNABAS.

In his second chapter this writer speaks thus:—

> "For he hath revealed to us by all the prophets that he needs neither sacrifices, nor burnt-offerings, nor oblations, saying thus, 'What is the multitude of your sacrifices unto me, saith the Lord? I am full of burnt-offerings, and desire not the fat of lambs, and the blood of bulls and goats, not when ye come to appear before me: for who hath required these things at your hands? Tread no more my courts, not though ye bring with you fine flour. Incense is a vain abomination unto me, and your new moons and Sabbaths I cannot endure.' He has therefore abolished these things, that the new law of our Lord Jesus Christ, which is without the yoke of necessity, might have a human oblation."

The writer may have intended to assert the abolition of the sacrifices only, as this was his special theme in this place. But he presently asserts the abolition of the Sabbath of the Lord. Here is his fifteenth chapter entire:—

> "Further, also, it is written concerning the Sabbath in the decalogue which [the Lord] spoke, face to face, to Moses on Mount Sinai, 'And sanctify ye the Sabbath of the Lord with clean hands and a pure heart.' And he says in another place, 'If my sons keep the Sabbath, then will I cause my mercy to rest upon them.' The Sabbath is mentioned at the beginning of the creation [thus]: 'And God made in six days the works of his hands, and made an end on the seventh day, and rested on it, and sanctified it.' Attend, my children, to the meaning of this expression, 'He finished in six days.' This implieth that the Lord will finish all things in six thousand years, for a day is with him a thousand years. And he himself testifieth, saying, 'Behold to-day will be as a thousand years.' Therefore, my children, in six days, that is, in six thousand years, all things will be finished. 'And he rested on the seventh day.' This meaneth: when his Son, coming [again], shall destroy the time of the wicked man, and judge the ungodly, and change

the sun, and the moon, and the stars, then shall he truly rest on the seventh day. Moreover, he says, 'Thou shalt sanctify it with pure hands and a pure heart.' If, therefore, any one can now sanctify the day which God hath sanctified, except he is pure in heart in all things, we are deceived. Behold, therefore: certainly then one properly resting sanctifies it, when we ourselves, having received the promise, wickedness no longer existing, and all things having been made new by the Lord, shall be able to work righteousness. Then we shall be able to sanctify it, having been first sanctified ourselves. Further, he says to them, 'Your new moons and your Sabbaths I cannot endure.' Ye perceive how he speaks: Your present Sabbaths are not acceptable to me, but that is which I have made [namely this], when, giving rest to all things, I shall make a beginning of the eighth day, that is, a beginning of another world. Wherefore, also, we keep the eighth day with joyfulness, the day, also, on which Jesus rose again from the dead. And when he had manifested himself, he ascended into the heavens."

Here are some very strange specimens of reasoning. The substance of what he says relative to the present observance of the Sabbath appears to be this: No one "can now sanctify the day which God hath sanctified except he is pure in heart in all things." But this cannot be the case until the present world shall pass away, "when we ourselves, having received the promise, wickedness no longer existing, and *all things having been made new* by the Lord, shall be able to work righteousness. Then we shall be able to sanctify it, having been first sanctified ourselves." Men cannot therefore keep the Sabbath while this wicked world lasts. And so he says, "Your present Sabbaths are not acceptable to me." That is to say, the keeping of the day which God has sanctified is not possible in such a wicked world. But though the seventh day cannot now be kept, the eighth day can be, and ought to be, because when the seventh thousand years are past there will be at the beginning of the eighth thousand the new creation. So the persons represented by this writer, do not attempt to keep the seventh day which God sanctified, for that is too pure to keep in this world, and can only be kept after the Saviour comes at the commencement of the seventh thousand years; but they "keep the eighth day with joyfulness, the day also on which Jesus rose again from the dead." Sunday, which God never sanctified, is exactly suitable for observance in the world as it now is. But the sanctified seventh day "we shall be able to sanctify" when all things have been made new. If our first-day friends think these words of some unknown writer of the second century more honorable to the first day of the week than to the seventh, they are welcome to them. Had the writer said, "It is easier to keep Sunday than the Sabbath while the world is so wicked," he would have stated the truth. But when in substance he says, "It is more acceptable to God to keep a common than a sanctified day while men are so sinful," he excuses his disobedience by uttering a falsehood. Several things however should be noted:—

1. In this quotation we have the reasons of a no-Sabbath man for keeping the festival of Sunday. It is not God's commandment, for there was none for that festi-

val; but the day God hallowed being too pure to keep while the world is so wicked, Sunday is therefore kept till the return of the Lord, and then the seventh day shall be truly sanctified by those who now regard it not.

2. But this writer, though saying what he is able in behalf of the first day of the week, applies to it no sacred name. He does not call it Christian Sabbath, nor Lord's day, but simply "the eighth day," and this because it succeeds the seventh day of the week.

3. It is also to be noticed that he expressly dates the Sabbath from the creation.

4. The change of the Sabbath was unknown to this writer. He kept the Sunday festival, not because it was purer than the sanctified seventh day, but because the seventh day was too pure to keep while the world is so wicked.

TESTIMONY OF THE EPISTLE OF PLINY.

Pliny was the Roman governor of Bithynia in the years 103 and 104. He wrote a letter to the emperor Trajan, in which he states what he had learned of the Christians as the result of examining them at his tribunal:—

> "They affirmed that the whole of their guilt or error was, that they met on a certain stated day [*stato die*], before it was light, and addressed themselves in a form of prayer to Christ, as to some God, binding themselves by a solemn oath, not for the purposes of any wicked design, but never to commit any fraud, theft, or adultery; never to falsify their word, nor deny a trust when they should be called upon to deliver it up; after which it was their custom to separate, and then reassemble to eat in common a harmless meal."—*Coleman's Ancient Christianity*, chap. i. sect. 1.

The letter of Pliny is often referred to as though it testified that the Christians of Bithynia celebrated the first day of the week. Yet such is by no means the case, as the reader can plainly see. Coleman says of it (page 528):—

> "This statement is evidence that these Christians kept a day as holy time, but whether it was the last, or the first day of the week, does not appear."

Such is the judgment of an able, candid, first-day church historian of good repute as a scholar. An anti-Sabbatarian writer of some repute speaks thus:—

> "As the Sabbath day appears to have been quite as commonly observed at this date as the Sun's day (if not even more so), it is just as probable that this 'stated day' referred to by Pliny was the *seventh* day, as that it was the *first* day; though the latter is generally taken for granted."—*Obligation of the Sabbath*, p. 300.

Every candid person must acknowledge that it is unjust to represent the letter of Pliny as testifying in behalf of the so-called Christian Sabbath. Next in order of time come the reputed epistles of Ignatius.

TESTIMONY OF THE EPISTLES OF IGNATIUS.

Of the fifteen epistles ascribed to Ignatius, eight are, by universal consent, accounted spurious; and eminent scholars have questioned the genuineness of the remaining seven. There are, however, two forms to these seven, a longer and a shorter, and while some doubt exists as to the shorter form, the longer form is by common consent ascribed to a later age than that of Ignatius. But the epistle to the Magnesians, which exists both in the longer and in the shorter form, is the one from which first-day writers obtain Ignatius' testimony in behalf of Sunday, and they quote for this both these forms. We therefore give both. Here is the shorter:—

> "For the divinest prophets lived according to Christ Jesus. On this account also they were persecuted, being inspired by his grace to fully convince the unbelieving that there is one God, who has manifested himself by Jesus Christ his Son, who is his eternal Word, not proceeding forth from silence, and who in all things pleased him that sent him. If, therefore, those who were brought up in the ancient order of things have come to the possession of a new hope, no longer observing the Sabbath, but living in the observance of the Lord's day, on which also our life has sprung again by him and by his death—whom some deny, by which mystery we have obtained faith, and therefore endure, that we may be found the disciples of Jesus Christ, our only master—how shall we be able to live apart from him, whose disciples the prophets themselves in the Spirit did wait for him as their teacher? And therefore he whom they rightly waited for, being come, raised them from the dead." Chaps. viii. and ix.

This paragraph is the one out of which a part of a sentence is quoted to show that Ignatius testifies in behalf of the Lord's-day festival, or Christian Sabbath. But the so-called Lord's day is only brought in by means of a false translation. This is the decisive sentence: μηκέτι σαββατίζοντες ἀλλὰ κατὰ κυριακὴν ζωὴν ζῶντες; literally: "no longer sabbatizing, but living according to Lord's life."

Eminent first-day scholars have called attention to this fact, and have testified explicitly that the term Lord's day has no right to appear in the translation; for the original is not κυριακὴν ἡμέραν, Lord's day, but κυριακὴν ζωήν, Lord's life. This is absolutely decisive, and shows that something akin to fraud has to be used in order to find a reference in this place to the so-called Christian Sabbath.

But there is another fact quite as much to the point. The writer was not speaking of those then alive, but of the ancient prophets. This is proved by the opening and closing words of the above quotation, which first-day writers always omit. The so-called Lord's day is inserted by a fraudulent translation; and now see what absurdity comes of it. The writer is speaking of the ancient prophets. If, therefore, the Sunday festival be inserted in this quotation from Ignatius he is made to declare that "the divinest prophets," who "were brought up in the ancient order of things," kept the first day and did not keep the Sabbath! Whereas, the truth is just the reverse of this. They certainly did keep the Sabbath, and did not keep the first day of the week. The writer speaks of the point when these men came "to the newness of hope," which must be their individual conversion to God. They certainly did observe and enforce the Sabbath after this act of conversion. See Isa., chaps. 56, 58; Jer. 17; Eze., chaps. 20, 22, 23. But they did also, as this writer truly affirms, live according to the Lord's life. The sense of the writer respecting the prophets must therefore be this: "No longer [after their conversion to God] observing the Sabbath [merely, as natural men] but living according to the Lord's life," or "according to Christ Jesus."

So much for the shorter form of the epistle to the Magnesians. Though the longer form is by almost universal consent of scholars and critics pronounced the work of some centuries after the time of Ignatius, yet as a portion of this also is often given by first-day writers to support Sunday, and given too as the words of Ignatius, we here present in full its reference to the first day of the week, and also to the Sabbath, which they generally omit. Here are its statements:—

> "Let us therefore no longer keep the Sabbath after the Jewish manner, and rejoice in days of idleness; for 'he that does not work, let him not eat.' For, say the [holy] oracles, 'In the sweat of thy face shalt thou eat thy bread.' But let every one of you keep the Sabbath after a spiritual manner, rejoicing in meditation on the law, not in relaxation of the body, admiring the workmanship of God, and not eating things prepared the day before, nor using lukewarm drinks, and walking within a prescribed space, nor finding delight in dancing and plaudits which have no sense in them. And after the observance of the Sabbath, let every friend of Christ keep the Lord's day as a festival, the resurrection day, the queen and chief of all the days [of the week]. Looking forward to this, the prophet declared, 'To the end, for the eighth day,' on which our life both sprang up again, and the victory over death was obtained in Christ," etc. Chapter ix.

This epistle, though the work of a later hand than that of Ignatius, is valuable for the light which it sheds upon the state of things when it was written. It gives us a correct idea of the progress of apostasy with respect to the Sabbath in the time of the writer. He speaks against Jewish superstition in the observance of the Sabbath, and condemns days of idleness as contrary to the declaration, "In the sweat of thy face shalt thou eat thy bread." But by days of idleness he cannot refer to the Sabbath, for this would be to make the fourth commandment clash with this text, whereas they must harmonize, inasmuch as they existed together during the former dispensation. Moreover, the Sabbath, though a day of abstinence from labor, is not a day of idleness, but of active participation in religious duties. He enjoins its observance after a spiritual manner. And after the Sabbath has been thus observed, "let every friend of Christ keep the Lord's day *as a festival*, the resurrection day, the queen and chief of all the days." The divine institution of the Sabbath was not yet done away, but the human institution of Sunday had become its equal, and was even commended above it. Not long after this, it took the whole ground, and the observance of the Sabbath was denounced as heretical and pernicious.

The reputed epistle of Ignatius to the Trallians in its shorter form does not allude to this subject. In its longer form, which is admitted to be the work of a later age than that of Ignatius, these expressions are found:—

> "During the Sabbath, he continued under the earth;" "at the dawning of the Lord's day he arose from the dead;" "the Sabbath embraces the burial; the Lord's day contains the resurrection." Chap. ix.

In the epistle to the Philippians, which is universally acknowledged to be the work of a later person than Ignatius, it is said:—

> "If any one fasts on the Lord's day or on the Sabbath, except on the paschal Sabbath only, he is a murderer of Christ." Chap. xiii.

We have now given every allusion to the Sabbath and first-day that can be found in any writing attributed to Ignatius. We have seen that the term "Lord's day" is not found in any sentence written by him. The first day is never called the Christian Sabbath, not even in the writings falsely attributed to him; nor is there in any of them a hint of the modern doctrine of the change of the Sabbath. Though falsely ascribed to Ignatius, and actually written in a later age, they are valuable in that they mark the progress of apostasy in the establishment of the Sunday festival. Moreover, they furnish conclusive evidence that the ancient Sabbath was retained for centuries in the so-called Catholic church, and that the Sunday festival was an institution entirely distinct from the Sabbath of the fourth commandment.

TESTIMONY OF THE CHURCH AT SMYRNA.

The epistle of Polycarp makes no reference to the Sabbath nor to the first day of the week. But "the encyclical epistle of the church at Smyrna concerning the martyrdom of the holy Polycarp," informs us that "the blessed Polycarp suffered martyrdom" "on the great Sabbath at the eighth hour." Chapter xxi. The margin says: "The great Sabbath is that before the passover." This day, thus mentioned, is not Sunday, but is the ancient Sabbath of the Lord.

TESTIMONY OF THE EPISTLE TO DIOGNETUS.

This was written by an unknown author, and Diognetus himself is known only by name, no facts concerning him having come down to us. It dates from the first part of the second century. The writer speaks of "the superstition as respects the Sabbaths" which the Jews manifested, and he adds these words: "To speak falsely of God, as if he forbade us to do what is good on the Sabbath days—how is not this impious?" But there is nothing in this to which a commandment-keeper would object, or which he might not freely utter.

The "Recognitions of Clement" is a kind of philosophical and theological romance. It purports to have been written by Clement of Rome, in the time of the apostle Peter, but was actually written "somewhere in the first half of the third century."

TESTIMONY OF THE RECOGNITIONS OF CLEMENT.

In book i., chapter xxxv., he speaks of the giving of the law thus:—

"Meantime they came to Mount Sinai, and thence the law was given to them with voices and sights from heaven, written in ten precepts, of which the first and greatest was that they should worship God himself alone," etc. In book iii., chapter lv., he speaks of these precepts as tests: "On account of those, therefore, who by neglect of their own salvation please the evil one, and those who by study of their own profit seek to please the good One, ten things have been prescribed as a test to this present age, according to the number of the ten plagues which were brought upon Egypt." In book ix., chapter xxviii., he says of the Hebrews, "that no child born among them is ever exposed, and that on every seventh day they all rest," etc. In book x., chap. lxxii., is given the conversion of one Faustinianus by St. Peter. And it is said, "He proclaimed a fast to all the people, and on the next Lord's day he baptized him."

This is all that I find in this work relating to the Sabbath and the so-called Lord's day. The writer held the ten commandments to be tests of character in the present dispensation. There is no reason to believe that he, or any other person in that age, held the Sunday festival as something to be observed in obedience to the fourth commandment.

TESTIMONY OF THE SYRIAC DOCUMENTS CONCERNING EDESSA.

On pages 35-55 of this work is given what purports to be "The Teaching of the Apostles." On page 36, the ascension of the Lord is said to have been upon the "first day of the week, and the end of the Pentecost." Two manifest falsehoods are here uttered; for the ascension was upon Thursday, and the Pentecost came ten days after the ascension. It is also said that the disciples came from Nazareth of Galilee to the mount of Olives on that selfsame day before the ascension, and yet that the ascension was "at the time of the early dawn." But Nazareth was distant from the mount of Olives at least sixty miles!

On page 38, a commandment from the apostles is given: "On the first [day] of the week, let there be service, and the reading of the holy Scriptures, and the oblation," because Christ arose on that day, was born on that day, ascended on that day, and will come again on that day. But here is one truth, one falsehood, and two mere assertions. The apostles are represented, on page 39, as commanding a fast of forty days, and they add: "Then celebrate the day of the passion [Friday], and the day of the resurrection," Sunday. But this would be only an annual celebration of these days.

And on pages 38 and 39 they are also represented as commanding service to be held on the fourth and sixth days of the week. The Sabbath is not mentioned in these "Documents," which were written about the commencement of the fourth century, when, in many parts of the world, that day had ceased to be hallowed.

CHAPTER IV.

TESTIMONY OF JUSTIN MARTYR.

Justin's "Apology" was written at Rome about the year 140. His "Dialogue with Trypho the Jew" was written some years later. In searching his works, we shall see how much greater progress apostasy had made at Rome than in the countries where those lived whose writings we have been examining. And yet nearly all these writings were composed at least a century later than those of Justin, though we have quoted them before quoting his, because of their asserted apostolic origin, or of their asserted origin within a few years of the times of the apostles.

It does not appear that Justin, and those at Rome who held with him in doctrine, paid the slightest regard to the ancient Sabbath. He speaks of it as abolished, and treats it with contempt. Unlike some whose writings have been examined, he denies that it originated at creation, and asserts that it was made in the days of Moses. He also differs with some already quoted in that he denies the perpetuity of the law of ten commandments. In his estimation, the Sabbath was a Jewish institution, absolutely unknown to good men before the time of Moses, and of no authority whatever since the death of Christ. The idea of the change of the Sabbath from the seventh day of the week to the first, is not only never found in his writings, but is absolutely irreconcilable with such statements as the foregoing, which abound therein. And yet Justin Martyr is prominently and constantly cited in behalf of the so-called Christian Sabbath.

The Roman people observed a festival on the first day of the week in honor of the sun. And so Justin in his Apology, addressed to the emperor of Rome, tells that monarch that the Christians met on "the day of the sun," for worship. He gives the day no sacred title, and does not even intimate that it was a day of abstinence from labor, only as they spent a portion of it in worship. Here are the words of his Apology on the Sunday festival:—

> "And on the day called Sunday, all who live in cities or in the country gather together to one place, and the memoirs of the apostles or the writings of the prophets are read, as long as time permits; then, when the reader has ceased, the president verbally instructs, and exhorts to the imitation of these good things. Then we all rise together and pray, and, as we before said, when our prayer is ended, bread and wine and water are brought, and the president in like manner offers prayers and thanksgivings, according to his ability, and the people assent, saying, Amen; and there

is a distribution to each, and a participation of that over which thanks have been given, and to those who are absent a portion is sent by the deacons. And they who are well to do, and willing, give what each thinks fit; and what is collected is deposited with the president, who succors the orphans and widows, and those who, through sickness or any other cause, are in want, and those who are in bonds, and the strangers sojourning among us, and, in a word, takes care of all who are in need. But Sunday is the day on which we all hold our common assembly, because it is the first day on which God, having wrought a change in the darkness and matter, made the world; and Jesus Christ our Saviour on the same day rose from the dead. For he was crucified on the day before that of Saturn (Saturday); and on the day after that of Saturn, which is the day of the sun, having appeared to his apostles and disciples, he taught them these things, which we have submitted to you also for your consideration." Chap. lxvii.

Not one word of this indicates that Justin considered the Sunday festival as a continuation of the Sabbath of the fourth commandment. On the contrary, he shows clearly that no such idea was cherished by him. For though the fourth commandment enjoins the observance of the seventh day because *God rested on that day* from the work of creation, Justin urged in behalf of the Sunday festival that it is *the day on which he began his work*. The honor paid to that festival was not therefore in Justin's estimation in any sense an act of obedience to the fourth commandment. He mentions as his other reason for the celebration by Christians of "the day of the sun," that the Saviour arose that day. But he claims no divine or apostolic precept for this celebration; the things which he says Christ taught his apostles being the doctrines which he had embodied in this Apology for the information of the emperor. And it is worthy of notice that though first-day writers assert that "Lord's day" was the familiar title of the first day of the week in the time of the Apocalypse, yet Justin, who is the first person after the sacred writers that mentions the first day, and this at a distance of only 44 years from the date of John's vision upon Patmos, does not call it by that title, but by the name which it bore as a heathen festival! If it be said that the term was omitted because he was addressing a heathen emperor, there still remains the fact that he mentions the day quite a number of times in his "Dialogue with Trypho," and yet never calls it "Lord's day," nor indeed does he call it by any name implying sacredness.

Now we present the statements concerning the Sabbath and first-day found in his "Dialogue with Trypho the Jew." The impropriety, not to say dishonesty, of quoting Justin in behalf of the modern doctrine of the change of the Sabbath, will be obvious to all. He was a most decided no-law, no-Sabbath writer, who used the day commonly honored as a festival by the Romans, as the most suitable, or most convenient, day for public worship, a position identical with that of modern no-Sabbath men. Justin may be called a law man in this sense, however, that while he abolishes the ten commandments, he calls the gospel "the new law." He is therefore really one who believes in the gospel and denies the law. But let us hear his own words. Trypho, having in chapter viii. advised Justin to observe the Sabbath, and "do all things which have been written in the law," in chapter x. says to him, "You observe no festivals or Sabbaths."

This was exactly adapted to bring out from Justin the answer that though he did not observe the seventh day as the Sabbath, he did thus rest on the first day, if it were true that that day was with him a day of abstinence from labor. And now observe Justin's answer given in chapter twelve:—

> "The new law requires you to keep perpetual Sabbath, and you, because you are idle for one day, suppose you are pious, not discerning why this has been commanded you; and if you eat unleavened bread, you say the will of God has been fulfilled. The Lord our God does not take pleasure in such observances: if there is any perjured person or a thief among you, let him cease to be so; if any adulterer, let him repent; then he has kept the sweet and true Sabbaths of God."

This language plainly implies that Justin held all days to be alike, and did not observe any one day as a day of abstinence from labor. But in chapter xviii., Justin asserts that the Sabbaths—and he doubtless includes the weekly with the annual—were enjoined upon the Jews for their wickedness:—

> "For we too would observe the fleshly circumcision, and the Sabbaths, and in short, all the feasts, if we did not know for what reason they were enjoined you—namely, on account of your transgressions and the hardness of your hearts. For if we patiently endure all things contrived against us by wicked men and demons, so that amid cruelties unutterable, death and torments, we pray for mercy to those who inflict such things upon us, and do not wish to give the least retort to any one, even as the new Law-giver commanded us: how is it, Trypho, that we would not observe those rites which do not harm us—I speak of fleshly circumcision, and Sabbaths, and feasts?"

Not only does he declare that the Jews were commanded to keep the Sabbath because of their wickedness, but in chapter xix. he denies that any Sabbath existed before Moses. Thus, after naming Adam, Abel, Enoch, Lot, and Melchizedek, he says:—

> "Moreover, all those righteous men already mentioned, though they kept no Sabbaths, were pleasing to God."

But though he thus denies the Sabbatic institution before the time of Moses, he presently makes this statement concerning the Jews:—

> "And you were commanded to keep Sabbaths, that you might retain the memorial of God. For his word makes this announcement, saying, 'That ye may know that I am God who redeemed you.'" [Eze. 20:12.]

The Sabbath is indeed the memorial of the God that made the heavens and the earth. And what an absurdity to deny that that memorial was set up when the creative work was done, and to affirm that twenty-five hundred years intervened between the work and the memorial!

In chapter xxi. Justin asserts "that God enjoined you [the Jews] to keep the Sabbath, and imposed on you other precepts for a sign, as I have already said, on account of your unrighteousness, and that of your fathers," &c., and quotes Ezekiel 20 to prove it. Yet that chapter declares that it was in order that they might know who was that being who sanctified them, *i. e.*, that they might know that their God was the Creator, that the Sabbath was made to them a sign.

In chapter xxiii., he again asserts that "in the times of Enoch" no one "observed Sabbaths." He then protests against Sabbatic observance as follows:—

> "Do you see that the elements are not idle, and keep no Sab-
> baths? Remain as you were born. For if there was no need of cir-
> cumcision before Abraham, or of the observance of Sabbaths, of
> feasts and sacrifices, before Moses; no more need is there of them
> now, after that, according to the will of God, Jesus Christ the Son
> of God has been born without sin, of a virgin sprung from the
> stock of Abraham."

That is to say, there was no Sabbatic institution before Moses, and neither is there any since Christ. But in chapter xxiv., Justin undertakes to bring in an argument for Sunday, not as a Sabbath, but as having greater mystery in it, and as being more honorable than the seventh day. Thus, alluding to circumcision on the eighth day of a child's life as an argument for the first-day festival, he says:—

> "It is possible for us to show how the eighth day possessed a
> certain mysterious import, which the seventh day did not possess,
> and which was promulgated by God through these rites."

That is to say, because God commanded the Hebrews to circumcise their children when they were eight days old, therefore all men should now esteem the first day of the week more honorable than the seventh day, which he commanded in the moral law, and which Justin himself, in chapter xix., terms "the memorial of God." In chapter xxvi., Justin says to Trypho that—

> "The Gentiles, who have believed on him, and have repented
> of the sins which they have committed, they shall receive the in-
> heritance along with the patriarchs and the prophets, and the just
> men who are descended from Jacob, even although they neither
> keep the Sabbath, nor are circumcised, nor observe the feasts."

And in proof of this, he quotes from Isa. 42, and 62, and 63, respecting the call of the Gentiles. Upon this (chapter xxvii.), Trypho the Jew very pertinently asks:—

> "Why do you select and quote whatever you wish from the
> prophetic writings, but do not refer to those which expressly com-
> mand the Sabbath to be observed? For Isaiah thus speaks [chap.
> 58:13, 14], 'If thou shalt turn away thy foot from the Sabbath,'" etc.

To which Justin makes this uncandid answer:—

> "I have passed them by, my friends, not because such prophecies were contrary to me, but because you have understood, and do understand, that although God commands you by all the prophets to do the same things which he also commanded by Moses, it was on account of the hardness of your hearts, and your ingratitude towards him, that he continually proclaims them, in order that, even in this way, if you repented, you might please him, and neither sacrifice your children to demons, nor be partakers with thieves," etc. And he adds: "So that, as in the beginning, these things were enjoined you because of your wickedness, in like manner, because of your steadfastness in it, or rather your increased proneness to it, by means of the same precepts, he calls you [by the prophets] to a remembrance or knowledge of it."

These are bitter words from a Gentile who had been a pagan philosopher, and they are in no sense a just answer unless it can be shown that the law was given to the Jews because they were so wicked, and was withheld from the Gentiles because they were so righteous. The truth is just the reverse of this. Eph. 2. But to say something against the Sabbath, Justin asks:—

> "Did God wish the priests to sin when they offer the sacrifices on the Sabbaths? or those to sin, who are circumcised and do circumcise on the Sabbaths; since he commands that on the eighth day—even though it happen to be a Sabbath—those who are born shall be always circumcised?" And he asks if the rite could not be one day earlier or later, and why those "who lived before Moses" "observed no Sabbaths?"

What Justin says concerning circumcision and sacrifices is absolutely without weight as an objection to the Sabbath, inasmuch as the commandment forbids, not the performance of religious duties, but our own work. Ex. 20:8-11. And his often repeated declaration that good men before the time of Moses did not keep the Sabbath, is mere assertion, inasmuch as God appointed it to a holy use in the time of Adam, and we do know of some in the patriarchal age who kept God's commandments, and were perfect before him.

In chapter xxix., Justin sneers at Sabbatic observance by saying, "Think it not strange that we drink hot water on the Sabbaths." And as arguments against the Sabbath he says that God "directs the government of the universe on this day equally as on all others," as though this were inconsistent with the present sacredness of the Sabbath, when it was also true that God thus governed the world in the period when Justin acknowledges the Sabbath to have been obligatory. And he again refers to the sacrifices and to those who lived in the patriarchal age.

In chapter xli., Justin again brings forward his argument for Sunday from circumcision:—

> "The command of circumcision, again, bidding [them] always circumcise the children on the eighth day, was a type of the true circumcision, by which we are circumcised from deceit and iniq

uity through Him who rose from the dead on the first day after the Sabbath [namely, through], our Lord Jesus Christ. For the first day after the Sabbath, remaining the first of all the days, is called, however, the eighth, according to the number of all the days of the cycle, and [yet] remains the first."

Sunday-keeping must be closely related to infant baptism, inasmuch as one of the chief arguments in modern times for the baptism of infants is drawn from the fact that God commanded the Hebrews to circumcise their male children; and Justin found his scriptural authority for first-day observance in the fact that this rite was to be performed when the child was eight days old! Yet this eighth day did not come on one day of the week, only, but on every day, and when it came on the seventh day it furnished Justin with an argument against the sacredness of the Sabbath! But let it come on what day of the week it might (and it came on all alike), it was an argument for Sunday! O wonderful *eighth* day, that can thrive on that which is positively fatal to the seventh, and that can come every week on the first day thereof, though there be only seven days in each week!

In chapters xliii., and xlvi., and xcii., Justin reiterates the assertion that those who lived in the patriarchal age did not hallow the Sabbath. But as he adds no new thought to what has been already quoted from him, these need not be copied.

But in chapter xlvii., we have something of interest. Trypho asks Justin whether those who believe in Christ, and obey him, but who wish to "observe these [institutions] will be saved?" Justin answers: "In my opinion, Trypho, such an one will be saved, if he does not strive in every way to persuade other men ... to observe the same things as himself, telling them that they will not be saved unless they do so." Trypho replied, "Why then have you said, 'In my opinion, such an one will be saved,' unless there are some who affirm that such will not be saved?"

In reply, Justin tells Trypho that there were those who would have no intercourse with, nor even extend hospitality to, such Christians as observed the law. And for himself he says: —

> "But if some, through weak-mindedness, wish to observe such institutions as were given by Moses (from which they expect some virtue, but which we believe were appointed by reason of the hardness of the people's hearts), along with their hope in this Christ, and [wish to perform] the eternal and natural acts of righteousness and piety, yet choose to live with the Christians and the faithful, as I said before, not inducing them either to be circumcised like themselves, or to keep the Sabbath, or to observe any other such ceremonies, then I hold that we ought to join ourselves to such, and associate with them in all things as kinsmen and brethren."

Justin's language shows that there were Sabbath-keeping Christians in his time. Such of them as were of Jewish descent no doubt generally retained circumcision. But it is very unjust in him to represent the Gentile Sabbath-keepers as observing this rite. That there were many of these is evident from the so-called

"Apostolical Constitutions," and even from the Ignatian Epistles. One good thing, however, Justin does say. The keeping of the commandments he terms the performance of "the eternal and natural acts of righteousness." He would consent to fellowship those who do these things provided they made them no test for others. He well knew in such case that the Sabbath would die out in a little time. Himself and the more popular party at Rome honored as their festival the day observed by the heathen Romans, as he reminds the emperor in his Apology, and he was willing to fellowship the Sabbath-keepers if they would not test him by the commandments, *i. e.*, if they would fellowship him in violating them.

That Justin held to the abrogation of the ten commandments is also manifest. Trypho, in the tenth chapter of the Dialogue, having said to Justin, "You do not obey his commandments," and again, "You do not observe the law," Justin answers in chapter xi. as follows:—

> "But we do not trust through Moses, or through the law; for then we would do the same as yourselves. But now—for I have read that there shall be a final law, and a covenant, the chiefest of all, which it is now incumbent on all men to observe, as many as are seeking after the inheritance of God. For the law promulgated on Horeb is now old, and belongs to yourselves alone; but this is for all universally. Now, law placed against law has abrogated that which is before it, and a covenant which comes after in like manner has put an end to the previous one."

We must, therefore, pronounce Justin a man who held to the abrogation of the ten commandments, and that the Sabbath was a Jewish institution which was unknown before Moses, and of no authority since Christ. He held Sunday to be the most suitable day for public worship, but not upon the ground that the Sabbath had been changed to it, for he cuts up the Sabbatic institution by the roots; and so far is he from calling this day the Christian Sabbath that he gives to it the name which it bore as a heathen festival.

CHAPTER V.

Irenæus—Dionysius—Melito—Bardesanes.

TESTIMONY OF IRENÆUS.

This father was born "somewhere between A. D. 120 and A. D. 140." He was "bishop of Lyons in France during the latter quarter of the second century," being ordained to that office "probably about A. D. 177." His work *Against Heresies* was written "between A. D. 182 and A. D. 188." First-day writers assert that Irenæus "says that the Lord's day was the Christian Sabbath." They profess to quote from him these words: "On the Lord's day every one of us Christians keeps the Sabbath, meditating on the law and rejoicing in the works of God."

No such language is found in any of the writings of this father. We will quote his entire testimony respecting the Sabbath and first-day, and the reader can judge. He speaks of Christ's observance of the Sabbath, and shows that he did not violate the day. Thus he says:—

> "It is clear, therefore, that he loosed and vivified those who believe in him as Abraham did, doing nothing contrary to the law when he healed upon the Sabbath day. For the law did not prohibit men from being healed upon the Sabbaths; [on the contrary] it even circumcised them upon that day, and gave command that the offices should be performed by the priests for the people; yea, it did not disallow the healing even of dumb animals. Both at Siloam and on frequent subsequent occasions, did he perform cures upon the Sabbath; and for this reason many used to resort to him on the Sabbath days. For the law commanded them to abstain from every servile work, that is, from all grasping after wealth which is procured by trading and by other worldly business; but it exhorted them to attend to the exercises of the soul, which consist in reflection, and to addresses of a beneficial kind for their neighbor's benefit. And therefore the Lord reproved those who unjustly blamed him for having healed upon the Sabbath days. For he did not make void, but fulfilled the law, by performing the offices of the high priest, propitiating God for men, and cleansing the lepers, healing the sick, and himself suffering death, that exiled man might go forth from condemnation, and might return without fear to his own inheritance. And again, the law did not forbid those who were hungry on the Sabbath days to take food lying ready at hand: it did, however, forbid them to reap and to gather into the barn." —*Against Heresies*, b. iv. chap. viii. sects. 2, 3.

The case of the priests on the Sabbath he thus presents:—

"And the priests in the temple profaned the Sabbath, and were blameless. Wherefore, then, were they blameless? Because when in the temple they were not engaged in secular affairs, but in the service of the Lord, fulfilling the law, but not going beyond it, as that man did, who of his own accord carried dry wood into the camp of God, and was justly stoned to death." Book iv. chap. viii. sect. 3.

Of the necessity of keeping the ten commandments, he speaks thus:—

"Now, that the law did beforehand teach mankind the necessity of following Christ, he does himself make manifest, when he replied as follows to him who asked him what he should do that he might inherit eternal life: 'If thou wilt enter into life, keep the commandments.' But upon the other asking, 'which?' again the Lord replied: 'Do not commit adultery, do not kill, do not steal, do not bear false witness, honor father and mother, and thou shalt love thy neighbor as thyself,'—setting as an ascending series before those who wished to follow him, the precepts of the law, as the entrance into life; and what he then said to one, he said to all. But when the former said, 'All these have I done' (and most likely he had not kept them, for in that case the Lord would not have said to him, 'Keep the commandments'), the Lord, exposing his covetousness, said to him, 'If thou wilt be perfect, go, sell all that thou hast, and distribute to the poor; and come follow me,' promising to those who would act thus, the portion belonging to the apostles.... But he taught that they should obey the commandments which God enjoined from the beginning, and do away with their former covetousness by good works, and follow after Christ." Book iv. chap. xii. sect. 5.

Irenæus certainly teaches a very different doctrine from that of Justin Martyr concerning the commandments. He believed that men must keep the commandments, in order to enter eternal life. He says further:—

"And [we must] not only abstain from evil deeds, but even from the desires after them. Now he did not teach us these things as being opposed to the law, but as fulfilling the law, and implanting in us the varied righteousness of the law. That would have been contrary to the law, if he had commanded his disciples to do anything which the law had prohibited." Book iv. chap. xiii. sect. 1.

He also makes the observance of the decalogue the test of true piety. Thus he says:—

"They (the Jews) had therefore a law, a course of discipline, and a prophecy of future things. For God at the first, indeed, warning them by means of natural precepts, which from the beginning he had implanted in mankind, that is, by means of the decalogue (which, if any one does not observe, he has no salvation), did then demand nothing more of them." Book iv. chap. xv. sect. 1.

The precepts of the decalogue he rightly terms "natural precepts," that is, precepts which constitute "the work of the law" written by nature in the hearts of all men, but marred by the presence of the carnal mind or law of sin in the members. That this law of God pertains alike to Jews and to Gentiles, he thus affirms:—

"Inasmuch, then, as all natural precepts are common to us and to them (the Jews), they had in them, indeed, the beginning and origin; but in us they have received growth and completion." Book iv. chap. xiii. sect. 4.

It is certain that Irenæus held the decalogue to be now binding on all men; for he says of it in the quotation above, "Which if any one does not observe, he has no salvation." But, though not consistent with his statement respecting the decalogue as the law of nature, he classes the Sabbath with circumcision, when speaking of it as a sign between God and Israel, and says, "The Sabbaths taught that we should continue day by day in God's service." "Moreover the Sabbath of God, that is, the kingdom, was, as it were, indicated by created things; in which [kingdom], the man who shall have persevered in serving God shall, in a state of rest, partake of God's table." He says also of Abraham that he was "without observance of Sabbaths." Book iv. chap. xvi. sects. 1, 2. But in the same chapter he again asserts the perpetuity and authority of the decalogue in these words:—

"Preparing man for this life, the Lord himself did speak in his own person to all alike the words of the decalogue; and therefore, in like manner, do they remain permanently with us, receiving, by means of his advent in the flesh, extension and increase, but not abrogation." Section 4.

This statement establishes the authority of each of the ten commandments in the gospel dispensation. Yet Irenæus seems to have regarded the fourth commandment as only a typical precept, and not of perpetual obligation like the others.

Irenæus regarded the Sabbath as something which pointed forward to the kingdom of God. Yet in stating this doctrine he actually indicates the origin of the Sabbath at creation, though, as we have seen, elsewhere asserting that it was not kept by Abraham. Thus, in speaking of the reward to be given the righteous, he says:—

"These are [to take place] in the times of the kingdom, that is, upon the seventh day, which has been sanctified, in which God rested from all the works which he created, which is the true Sabbath of the righteous, in which they shall not be engaged in any earthly occupation; but shall have a table at hand prepared for them by God, supplying them with all sorts of dishes." Book v. chap. xxxiii. sect. 2. And he elsewhere says: "In as many days as this world was made, in so many thousand years shall it be concluded.... For the day of the Lord is as a thousand years: and in six days created things were completed: it is evident, therefore, that they will come to an end at the sixth thousand year." Book v. chap. xxviii. sect. 3.

Though Irenæus is made by first-day writers to bear a very explicit testimony that Sunday is the Christian Sabbath, the following, which constitutes the seventh fragment of what is called the "Lost Writings of Irenæus," is the only instance which I have found in a careful search through all his works in which he even mentions the first day. Here is the entire first-day testimony of this father:—

> "This [custom], of not bending the knee upon Sunday, is a symbol of the resurrection, through which we have been set free, by the grace of Christ, from sins, and from death, which has been put to death under him. Now this custom took its rise from apostolic times, as the blessed Irenæus, the martyr and bishop of Lyons, declares in his treatise *On Easter*, in which he makes mention of Pentecost also; upon which [feast] we do not bend the knee, because it is of equal significance with the Lord's day, for the reason already alleged concerning it."

This is something very remarkable. It is not what Irenæus said, after all, but is what an unknown writer, in a work entitled *Quæs. et Resp. ad Othod.*, says of him. And all that this writer says of Irenæus is that he declares the custom of not kneeling upon Sunday "took its rise from apostolic times"! It does not even appear that Irenæus even used the term Lord's day as a title for the first day of the week. Its use in the present quotation is by the unknown writer to whom we are indebted for the statement here given respecting Irenæus. And this writer, whoever he be, is of the opinion that the Pentecost is of equal consequence with the so-called Lord's day! And well he may so judge, inasmuch as both of these Catholic festivals are only established by the authority of the church. The testimony of Irenæus in behalf of Sunday does therefore amount simply to this: That the resurrection is to be commemorated by "not bending the knee upon Sunday"!

The fiftieth fragment of the "Lost Writings of Irenæus" is derived from the Nitrian Collection of Syriac MSS. It relates to the resurrection of the dead. In a note appended to it the Syriac editor says of Irenæus that he "wrote to an Alexandrian to the effect that it is right, with respect to the feast of the resurrection, that we should celebrate it upon the first day of the week." No extant writing of Irenæus contains this statement, but it is likely that the Syriac editor possessed some portion of his works now lost. And here again it is worthy of notice that we have from Irenæus only the plain name of "first day of the week." As to the manner of celebrating it, the only thing which he sets forth is "not bending the knee upon Sunday."

In the thirty-eighth fragment of his "Lost Writings" he quotes Col. 2:16, but whether with reference to the seventh day, or merely respecting the ceremonial sabbaths, his comments do not determine. We have now given every statement of Irenæus which bears upon the Sabbath and the Sunday. It is manifest that the advocates of first-day sacredness have made Irenæus testify in its behalf to suit themselves. He alludes to the first day of the week once or twice, but never uses for it the title of Lord's day or Christian Sabbath, and the *only* thing which he mentions as entering into the celebration of the festival was that Christians should not kneel in prayer on that day! By first-day writers, Irenæus is made to bear an explicit testimony that Sunday is the Lord's day and the Christian Sabbath! And to give great weight to this alleged fact, they say that he was the disciple of Polycarp, who was the disciple of John: and whereas John speaks of the Lord's day, Irenæus, who must have known what he meant by the term, says that the Lord's day is the first day of the week! But Polycarp, in his epistle, does not even mention the first day of the week, and Irenæus, in his extended writings, mentions it only twice, and that in "lost fragments," preserved at secondhand, and in neither instance does he call it any thing but plain "first day of the week"! And the only honor which he mentions as due this day is that the knee should not be bent upon it! And even this was not spoken of every Sunday in the year, but only of "Easter Sunday," the anniversary of Christ's resurrection!

Here we might dismiss the case of Irenæus. But our first-day friends are determined at least to connect him with the use of Lord's day as a name for Sunday. They therefore bring forward Eusebius, who wrote 150 years later, to prove that Irenæus did call Sunday by that name. Eusebius alludes to the controversy in the time of Irenæus, respecting the *annual* celebration of Christ's resurrection in what was called the festival of the passover. He says (Eccl. Hist., b. v. chap. xxiii.) that the bishops of different countries, and Irenæus was of the number, decreed "that the mystery of our Lord's resurrection should be celebrated on no other day than the Lord's day; and that on this day alone we should observe the close of the paschal fasts," and not on the fourteenth of the first month as practiced by the other party. And in the next chapter, Eusebius represents Irenæus as writing a letter to this effect to the Bishop of Rome. But observe, Eusebius does not quote the words of any of these bishops, but simply gives their decisions in his own language. There is therefore no proof that they used the term Lord's day instead of first day of the week. But we have evidence that in the decision of this case which Irenæus sent forth, he used the term "first day of the week." For the introduction to the fiftieth fragment of his "Lost Writings," already quoted, gives an ancient statement of his words in this decision, as plain "first day of the week." It is Eusebius who gives us the term Lord's day in recording what was said by these bishops concerning the first day of the week. In his time, A. D. 324, Lord's day had become a common designation of Sunday. But it was not such in the time of Irenæus, A. D. 178. We have found no writer who flourished before him who applies it to Sunday; it is not so applied by Irenæus; and we shall find no decisive instance of such use till the close of the second century.

TESTIMONY OF DIONYSIUS, BISHOP OF CORINTH.

This father, about A. D. 170, wrote a letter to the Roman church, in which are found these words:—

"We passed this holy Lord's day, in which we read your letter, from the constant reading of which we shall be able to draw

admonition, even as from the reading of the former one you sent
us written through Clement."

This is the earliest use of the term Lord's day to be found in the fathers. But
it cannot be called a decisive testimony that Sunday was thus known at this date,
inasmuch as every writer who precedes Dionysius calls it "first day of the week,"
"eighth day," or "Sunday," but never once by this title; and Dionysius says nothing to indicate that Sunday was intended, or to show that he did not refer to that
day which alone has the right to be called the Lord's "holy day." Isa. 58:13. We
have found several express testimonies to the sacredness of the Sabbath in the
writers already examined.

TESTIMONY OF MELITO, BISHOP OF SARDIS.

This father wrote about A. D. 177. We know little of this writer except the titles
of his books, which Eusebius has preserved to us. One of these titles is this: "On
the Lord's Day." But it should be remembered that down to this date no writer
has called Sunday the Lord's day; and that every one who certainly spoke of that
day called it by some other name than Lord's day. To say, therefore, as do first-
day writers, that Melito wrote of Sunday, is to speak without just warrant. He
uses τῆς κυριακῆς, "the Lord's," but does not join with it ἡμέρα, a "day," as does
John. He wrote of something pertaining to the Lord, but it is not certain that it was
the Lord's day. Moreover, Clement, who next uses this term, uses it in a mystical
sense.

TESTIMONY OF THE HERETIC BARDESANES.

Bardesanes, the Syrian, flourished about A. D. 180. He belonged to the Gnostic
sect of Valentinians, and abandoning them, "devised errors of his own." In his
"Book of the Laws of Countries," he replies to the views of astrologers who assert
that the stars govern men's actions. He shows the folly of this by enumerating the
peculiarities of different races and sects. In doing this, he speaks of the strictness
with which the Jews kept the Sabbath. Of the new sect called Christians, which
"Christ at his advent planted in every country," he says:—

"On one day, the first of the week, we assemble ourselves together, and on the days of the readings we abstain from [taking]
sustenance."

This shows that the Gnostics used Sunday as the day for religious assemblies.
Whether he recognized others besides Gnostics, as Christians, we cannot say. We
find no allusion, however, to Sunday as a day of abstinence from labor, except
so far as necessary for their meetings. What their days of fasting, which are here
alluded to, were, cannot now be determined. It is also worthy of notice that this
writer, who certainly speaks of Sunday, and this as late as A. D. 180, does not call
it Lord's day, nor give it any sacred title whatever, but speaks of it as "first day of
the week." No writer down to A. D. 180, who is known to speak of Sunday, calls
it the Lord's day.

CHAPTER VI.

Theophilus—Clement of Alexandria.

TESTIMONY OF THEOPHILUS OF ANTIOCH.

THIS father became Bishop of Antioch in A. D. 168, and died A. D. 181. First-day writers represent him as saying, "Both *custom* and *reason* challenge from us that we should honor the Lord's day, seeing on that day it was that our Lord Jesus completed his resurrection from the dead." These writers, however, give no reference to the particular place in the works of Theophilus where this is to be found. I have carefully examined every paragraph of all the extant writings of this father, and that several times over, without discovering any such statement. I am constrained, therefore, to state that nothing of the kind above quoted is to be found in Theophilus! And further than this, the term Lord's day does not occur in this writer, nor does he even refer to the first day of the week except in quoting Genesis 1, in a *single instance*! But though he makes no mention of the Sunday festival, he makes the following reference to the Sabbath in his remarks concerning the creation of the world:—

> "Moreover [they spoke], concerning the seventh day, which
> all men acknowledge; but the most know not that what among
> the Hebrews is called the 'Sabbath,' is translated into Greek the
> 'seventh' (ἑβδομὰς), a name which is adopted by every nation,
> although they know not the reason of the appellation." *Theophilus
> to Autolycus*, b. ii. chap. xii.

Though Theophilus is in error in saying that the Hebrew word *Sabbath* is translated into Greek *seventh*, his statement indicates that he held the origin of the Sabbath to be when God sanctified the seventh day. These are the words of Scripture, as given by him, on which he wrote the above:—

> "And on the sixth day God finished his works which he made,
> and rested on the seventh day from all his works which he made.
> And God blessed the seventh day, and sanctified it; because in it
> he rested from all his works which God began to create." Book ii.
> chap. xi.

In the fifteenth chapter of this book, he compares those who "keep the law and commandments of God" to the fixed stars, while the "wandering stars" are "a type of the men who have wandered from God, abandoning his law and commandments." Of the law itself, he speaks thus:—

"We have learned a holy law; but we have as law-giver him who is really God, who teaches us to act righteously, and to be pious, and to do good." After quoting all but the third and fourth commandments, he says: "Of this great and wonderful law which tends to all righteousness, the TEN HEADS are such as we have already rehearsed." Book iii. chap. ix.

He makes the keeping of the law and commandments the condition of a part in the resurrection to eternal life: —

"For God has given us a law and holy commandments; and every one who keeps these can be saved, and, obtaining the resurrection, can inherit incorruption." Book ii. chap. xxvii.

And yet this man who bears such a noble testimony to the commandments and the law, and who says not one word concerning the festival of Sunday, is made to speak explicitly in behalf of this so-called Christian Sabbath!

TESTIMONY OF CLEMENT OF ALEXANDRIA, A. D. 194.

This father was born about A. D. 160, and died about A. D. 220. He wrote about A. D. 194, and is the first of the fathers who uses the term Lord's day in such a manner as possibly to signify by it the first day of the week. And yet he expressly speaks of the Sabbath as a day of rest, and of the first day of the week as a day for labor! The change of the Sabbath and the institution of the so-called Christian Sabbath were alike unknown to him. Of the ten commandments, he speaks thus: —

"We have the decalogue given by Moses, which, indicating by an elementary principle, simple and of one kind, defines the designation of sins in a way conducive to salvation," etc. — *The Instructor*, b. iii. chap. xii.

He thus alludes to the Sabbath: —

"Thus the Lord did not hinder from doing good while keeping the Sabbath; but allowed us to communicate of those divine mysteries, and of that holy light, to those who are able to receive them." — *The Miscellanies*, b. i. chap. i.

"To restrain one's self from doing good is the work of vice; but to keep from wrong is the beginning of salvation. So the Sabbath, by abstinence from evils, seems to indicate self-restraint." Book iv. chap. iii.

He calls love the Lord of the Sabbath: —

"He convicted the man, who boasted that he had fulfilled the injunctions of the law, of not loving his neighbor; and it is by beneficence that the love which, according to the Gnostic ascending scale, is Lord of the Sabbath, proclaims itself." Book iv. chap. vi.

Referring to the case of the priests in Eze. 43:27, he says: —

"And they purify themselves seven days, the period in which

creation was consummated. For on the seventh day the rest is celebrated; and on the eighth, he brings a propitiation, as it is written in Ezekiel, according to which propitiation the promise is to be received." Book iv. chap. xxv.

We come now to the first instance in the fathers in which the term Lord's day is perhaps applied to Sunday. Clement is the father who does this, and he very properly substantiates it with evidence. He does not say that Saint John thus applied this name, but he finds authority for this in the writings of the heathen philosopher Plato, who, he thinks, spoke of it prophetically!

"And the Lord's day Plato prophetically speaks of in the tenth book of the *Republic,* in these words: 'And when seven days have passed to each of them in the meadow, on the eighth day they are to set out and arrive in four days.' By the meadow is to be understood the fixed sphere, as being a mild and genial spot, and the locality of the pious; and by the seven days each motion of the seven planets, and the whole practical art which speeds to the end of the rest. But after the wandering orbs the journey leads to Heaven, that is, to the eighth motion and day. And he says that souls are gone on the fourth day, pointing out the passage through the four elements." Book v. chap. xiv.

By the eighth day to which Clement here applies the name of Lord's day the first day is possibly intended, though he appears to speak solely of mystical days. But having said thus much in behalf of the eighth day, he in the very next sentence commences to establish from the Greek writers the sacredness of that seventh day which the Hebrews hallowed. This shows that whatever regard he might have for the eighth day, he certainly cherished the seventh day as sacred. Thus he continues: —

"But the seventh day is recognized as sacred, not by the Hebrews only, but also by the Greeks; according to which the whole world of all animals and plants revolves. Hesiod says of it: —

"'The first, and fourth, and seventh days were held sacred.'

"And again: 'And on the seventh the sun's resplendent orb.'

"And Homer: 'And on the seventh then came the sacred day.'

"And: 'The seventh was sacred.'

"And again: 'It was the seventh day, and all things were accomplished.'

"And again: 'And on the seventh morn we leave the stream of Acheron.'

"Callimachus the poet also writes: 'It was the seventh morn, and they had all things done.'

"And again: 'Among good days is the seventh day, and the seventh race.'

"And: 'The seventh is among the prime, and the seventh is perfect.'

"And:

'Now all the seven were made in starry heaven,
In circles shining as the years appear.'

"The Elegies of Solon, too, intensely deify the seventh day."
Book v. chap. xiv.

Some of these quotations are not now found in the writings which Clement cites. And whether or not he rightly applies them to the seventh-day Sabbath, the fact that he does so apply them is incontestible proof that he honored that day as sacred, whatever might also be his regard for that day which he distinguishes as the eighth.

In book vi., chapter v., he alludes to the celebration of some of the annual sabbaths. And in chapter xvi., he thus speaks of the fourth commandment: —

"And the fourth word is that which intimates that the world was created by God, and that *he gave us the seventh day as a rest*, on account of the trouble that there is in life. For God is incapable of weariness, and suffering, and want. *But we who bear flesh need rest. The seventh day, therefore, is proclaimed a rest*—abstraction from ills—preparing for the primal day, our true rest; which, in truth, is the first creation of light, in which all things are viewed and possessed. From this day the first wisdom and knowledge illuminate us."

This certainly teaches that the Sabbath was made for man, and that he now needs it as a day of rest. It also indicates that Clement recognized the authority of the fourth commandment, for he treats of the ten commandments in order, and comments on what each enjoins or forbids. In the next paragraph, however, he makes some remarkable suggestions. Thus he says: —

"Having reached this point, we must mention these things by the way; since the discourse has turned on the seventh and the eighth. For the eighth may possibly turn out to be properly the seventh, and the seventh, manifestly the sixth, and the latter,[4] properly the Sabbath, and the seventh, a day of work. For the creation of the world was concluded in six days." Book vi. chap. xvi.

Clement thinks it possible that the eighth day (Sunday), may really be the seventh day, and that the seventh day (Saturday) may in fact be the true sixth day. But let not our Sunday friends exult at this, for Clement by no means helps their

[4] We notice that one first-day writer is so determined that Clement shall testify in behalf of Sunday, that he deliberately changes his words. Instead of giving his words as they are, thus: "the *latter*, properly the Sabbath," in which case, as the connection shows, Saturday is the day intended, he gives them thus: "The *eighth*, properly the Sabbath," thereby making him call Sunday the Sabbath. This is a remarkable fraud, but it shows that the words as written by Clement could not be made to uphold Sunday. See "The Lord's Day," by Rev. G. H. Jenks, p. 50.

case. Having said that Sunday may be properly the seventh day, and Saturday manifestly the sixth day, he calls "the LATTER properly the Sabbath, and the seventh a day of work"! By "the latter," of necessity must be understood the day last mentioned, which he says should be called not the seventh, but the sixth; and by "the seventh," must certainly be intended that day which he says is not the eighth, but the seventh, that is to say, Sunday. It follows therefore in the estimation of Clement that Sunday was a day of ordinary labor, and Saturday, the day of rest. He had an excellent opportunity to say that the eighth day or Sunday was not only the seventh day, but also the true Sabbath, but instead of doing this he gives this honor to the day which he says is not the seventh but the sixth, and declares that the real seventh day or Sunday is "a day of work." And he proceeds at length to show the sacredness and importance of the number six. His opinion of the numbering of the days is unimportant; but the fact that this father who is the first writer that connects the term Lord's day with the eighth day or Sunday, does expressly represent that day as one of ordinary labor, and does also give to the previous day the honors of the Sabbath is something that should shut the mouths of those who claim him as a believer in the so-called Christian Sabbath.

In the same chapter, this writer alludes to the Sabbath vaguely, apparently understanding it to prefigure the rest that remains to the people of God:—

> "Rightly, then, they reckon the number seven motherless and childless, interpreting the Sabbath, and figuratively expressing the nature of the rest, in which 'they neither marry nor are given in marriage any more.'"

The following quotation completes the testimony of Clement. He speaks of the precept concerning fasting, that it is fulfilled by abstinence from sinful pleasure. And thus he says:—

> "He fasts, then, according to the law, abstaining from bad deeds, and, according to the perfection of the gospel, from evil thoughts. Temptations are applied to him, not for his purification, but, as we have said, for the good of his neighbors, if, making trial of toils and pains, he has despised and passed them by. The same holds of pleasure. For it is the highest achievement for one who has had trial of it, afterwards to abstain. For what great thing is it, if a man restrains himself in what he knows not? He, in fulfillment of the precept, according to the gospel, keeps the Lord's day, when he abandons an evil disposition, and assumes that of the Gnostic, glorifying the Lord's resurrection in himself." Book vii. chap. xii.

Clement asserts that one fasts according to the law when he abstains from evil deeds, and, according to the gospel, when he abstains from evil thoughts. He shows how the precept respecting fasting is fulfilled when he speaks of one who "in fulfillment of the precept, according to the gospel, keeps the Lord's day when he abandons an evil disposition." This abandonment of an evil disposition, according to Clement, keeps the Lord's day, and glorifies the Lord's resurrection.

But this duty pertains to no one day of the week, but to all alike, so that he seems evidently to inculcate a perpetual Lord's day, even as Justin Martyr enjoins the observance of a "perpetual Sabbath," to be acceptably sanctified by those who maintain true repentance. Though these writers are not always consistent with themselves, yet two facts go to show that Clement in this book means just what his words literally import, viz., that the keeping of the Lord's day and the glorifying of the resurrection is not the observance of a certain day of the week, but the performance of a work which embraces every day of one's whole life.

1. The first of these facts is his express statement of this doctrine in the first paragraph of the seventh chapter of this book. Thus he says:—

> "Now, we are commanded to reverence and to honor the same one, being persuaded that he is Word, Saviour, and Leader, and by him, the Father, NOT ON SPECIAL DAYS, AS SOME OTHERS, but *doing this continually in our whole life*, and in every way. Certainly the elect race, justified by the precept, says, 'Seven times a day have I praised thee.' Whence *not* in a specified place, or selected temple, or at *certain festivals*, and on *appointed days*, but *during his whole life*, the Gnostic in every place, even if he be alone by himself, and wherever he has any of those who have exercised the like faith, honors God; that is, acknowledges his gratitude for the knowledge of the way to live." Book vii. chap. vii.

2. The second of these facts is that in book vi., chapter xvi., as already quoted, he expressly represents Sunday as "a day of work."

Certainly Clement of Alexandria should not be cited as teaching the change of the Sabbath, or advocating the so-called Christian Sabbath.

CHAPTER VII.

TESTIMONY OF TERTULLIAN, A. D. 200.

THIS writer contradicts himself in the most extraordinary manner concerning the Sabbath and the law of God. He asserts that the Sabbath was abolished by Christ, and elsewhere emphatically declares that he did not abolish it. He says that Joshua violated the Sabbath, and then expressly declares that he did not violate it. He says that Christ broke the Sabbath, and then shows that he never did this. He represents the eighth day as more honorable than the seventh, and elsewhere states just the reverse. He asserts that the law is abolished, and in other places affirms its perpetual obligation. He speaks of the Lord's day as the eighth day, and is the second of the early writers who makes an application of this term to Sunday, if we allow Clement to have really spoken of it. But though he thus uses the term like Clement he also like him teaches a perpetual Lord's day, or, like Justin Martyr, a perpetual Sabbath in the observance of every day. And with the observance of Sunday as the Lord's day he brings in "offerings for the dead" and the perpetual use of the sign of the cross. But he expressly affirms that these things rest, not upon the authority of the Scriptures, but wholly upon that of tradition and custom. And though he speaks of the Sabbath as abrogated by Christ, he expressly contradicts this by asserting that Christ "did not at all rescind the Sabbath," and that he imparted an additional sanctity to that day which from the beginning had been consecrated by the benediction of the Father. This strange mingling of light and darkness plainly indicates the age in which this author lived. He was not so far removed from the time of the apostles but that many clear rays of divine truth shone upon him; and he was far enough advanced in the age of apostasy to have its dense darkness materially affect him. He stood on the line between expiring day and advancing night. Sometimes the law of God was unspeakably sacred; at other times tradition was of higher authority than the law. Sometimes divine institutions were alone precious in his estimation; at others he was better satisfied with those which were sustained only by custom and tradition.

Tertullian's first reference to Sunday is found in that part of his Apology in which he excuses his brethren from the charge of sun-worship. Thus he says:—

"Others, again, certainly with more information and greater verisimilitude, believe that the sun is our God. We shall be counted Persians, perhaps, though we do not worship the orb of day painted on a piece of linen cloth, having himself everywhere in his own disk. The idea, no doubt, has originated from our being known to turn to the east in prayer. But you, many of you, also, under pretense sometimes of worshiping the heavenly bodies, move your lips in the direction of the sunrise. In the same way, if we devote Sunday to rejoicing, from a far different reason than sun-worship, we have some resemblance to those of you who devote the day of Saturn to ease and luxury, though they, too, go far away from Jewish ways, of which indeed they are ignorant."—*Thelwell's Translation*, sect. 16.

Several important facts are presented in this quotation.

1. Sunday was an ancient heathen festival in honor of the sun.

2. Those Christians who observed the festival of Sunday were claimed by the heathen as sun-worshipers.

3. The entrance of the Sunday festival into the church in an age of apostasy when men very generally honored it, was not merely not difficult to be effected, it was actually difficult to be prevented.

It would seem from the closing sentence that some of the heathen used the seventh day as a day of ease and luxury. But Mr. Reeve's Translation gives a very different sense. He renders Tertullian thus:—

> "We solemnize the day after Saturday in contradistinction to those who call this day their Sabbath, and devote it to ease and eating, deviating from the old Jewish customs, which they are now very ignorant of."

The persons here mentioned so contemptuously could not be heathens, for they do not call any day "their Sabbath." Nor could they be Jews, as is plain from the form of expression used. If we accept Mr. Reeve's Translation, these persons were Christians who observe the seventh day. Tertullian does not say that the Sunday festival was observed by divine authority, but that they might distinguish themselves from those who call the seventh day the Sabbath.

Tertullian again declares that his brethren did not observe the days held sacred by the Jews.

> "We neither accord with the Jews in their peculiarities in regard to food, nor in their sacred days."—*Apology*, sect. 21.

But those Christians who would not keep the Sabbath because the festival of Sunday was in their estimation more worthy of honor, or more convenient to observe, were greatly given to the observance of other days, in common with the heathen, besides Sunday. Thus Tertullian charges home upon them this sin:—

> "The Holy Spirit upbraids the Jews with their holy days. 'Your sabbaths, and new moons, and ceremonies,' says he, 'my soul hateth.' By us (to whom Sabbaths are strange, and the new moons, and festivals formerly beloved by God) the Saturnalia and New Year's and mid-winter's festivals and Matronalia are frequented—presents come and go—New Year's gifts—games join their noise—banquets join their din! Oh! better fidelity of the nations

to their own sect, which claims no solemnity of the Christians for itself! Not the Lord's day, not Pentecost, even if they had known them, would they have shared with us; for they would fear lest they should seem to be Christians. *We* are not apprehensive lest we seem to be *heathens*! If any indulgence is to be granted to the flesh, you have it. I will not say your own days, but more too; for to the *heathens* each festive day occurs but once annually; *you* have a festive day every eighth day." —*On Idolatry*, chap. xiv.

These Sunday-festival Christians, "to whom Sabbaths" were "strange," could not have kept Sunday as a Sabbath. They had never heard that by divine authority the Sabbath was changed from the seventh to the first day of the week, and that Sunday is the Christian Sabbath. Let any candid man read the above words from Tertullian, and then deny, if he can, that these strangers to the Sabbath, and observers of heathen festivals, were not a body of apostatizing Christians!

Hereafter Tertullian will give an excellent commentary on his quotation from Isaiah. It seems from him that the so-called Lord's day came once in eight days. Were these words to be taken in their most obvious sense, then it would come one day later each week than it did the preceding week, and thus it would come successively on all the days of the week in order, at intervals of eight days. He might in such case well say: —

"However, *every* day is the Lord's; every hour, every time, is apt for baptism; if there is a difference in the *solemnity*, in the *grace*, distinction there is none." —*On Baptism*, chap. xix.

But it seems that Tertullian by the eighth day intended Sunday. And here is something from him relative to the manner of keeping it. Thus he says: —

"In the matter of *kneeling* also, prayer is subject to diversity of observance, through the act of some few who abstain from kneeling on the Sabbath; and since this dissension is particularly on its trial before the churches, the Lord will give his grace that the dissentients may either yield, or else indulge their opinion without offense to others. We, however (just as we have received), only on the day of the Lord's resurrection ought to guard not only against kneeling, but every posture and office of solicitude; deferring even our businesses, lest we give any place to the devil. Similarly, too, in the period of Pentecost; which period we distinguish by the same solemnity of exultation. But who would hesitate *every* day to prostrate himself before God, at least in the first prayer with which we enter on the daylight." —*On Prayer*, chap. xxiii.

A more literal translation of this passage would expressly connect the term Lord's day with the day of Christ's resurrection, the original being "die Dominico resurrexionis." The special weekly honor which Tertullian would have men confer solely upon Sunday was to pray on that day in a *standing* posture. And somewhat to his annoyance, "some few" would thus act with reference to the Sabbath. There is, however, some reference to the deferral of business on Sunday. And this is worthy of notice, for it is the first sentence we have discovered that looks like abstinence from labor on Sunday, and we shall not find another before the time of Constantine's famous Sunday law, A. D. 321.

But this passage is far from asserting that labor on Sunday was sinful. It speaks of "deferring even our businesses;" but this does not necessarily imply anything beyond its postponement during the hours devoted to religious services. And we shall find nothing in Tertullian, nor in his cotemporaries, that will go beyond this, while we shall find much to restrict us to the interpretation of his words here given. Tertullian could not say that Sabbaths were strange to him and his brethren if they religiously refrained from labor on each Sunday. But let us hear him again concerning the observance of Sunday and kindred practices: —

"We take also, in meetings before daybreak, and from the hand of none but the presidents, the sacrament of the Eucharist, which the Lord both commanded to be eaten at meal-times, and enjoined to be taken by all [alike]. As often as the anniversary comes round, we make offerings for the dead as birth-day honors. We count fasting or kneeling in worship on the Lord's day to be unlawful. We rejoice in the same privilege also from Easter to Whit-sunday. We feel pained should any wine or bread, even though our own, be cast upon the ground. At every forward step and movement, at every going in and out, when we put on our clothes and shoes, when we bathe, when we sit at table, when we light the lamps, on couch, on seat, in all the ordinary actions of daily life, we trace upon the forehead the sign [of the cross].

"If, for these and other such rules, you insist upon having positive Scripture injunction, you will find none. Tradition will be held forth to you as the originator of them, custom, as their strengthener, and faith, as their observer. That reason will support tradition, and custom, and faith, you will either yourself perceive, or learn from some one who has." —*De Corona*, sects. 3 and 4.

The things which he counted unlawful on Sunday he expressly names. These are fasting and kneeling on that day. But ordinary labor does not come into his list of things unlawful on that day. And now observe what progress apostasy and superstition had made in other things also. "Offerings for the dead" were regularly made, and the sign of the cross was repeated as often as God would have men rehearse his commandments. See Deut. 6:6-9. And now if you wish to know Tertullian's authority for the Sunday festival, offerings for the dead, and the sign of the cross, he frankly tells you what it is. He had no authority from the Scriptures. Custom and tradition were all that he could offer. Modern divines can find plenty of authority, from the Scriptures, as they assert, for maintaining the so-called Lord's day. Tertullian knew of none. He took the Sunday festival, offerings for the dead, and the sign of the cross, on the authority of custom and tradition; if you take the first on such authority, why do you not, also, the other two?

But Tertullian finds it necessary to write a second defense of his brethren from the charge of being sun-worshipers, a charge directly connected with their observance of the festival of Sunday. Here are his words:—

> "Others, with greater regard to good manners, it must be confessed, suppose that the sun is the god of the Christians, because it is a well-known fact that we pray towards the east, or because we make Sunday a day of festivity. What then? Do you do less than this? Do not many among you, with an affectation of sometimes worshiping the heavenly bodies likewise, move your lips in the direction of the sunrise? It is you, at all events, who have even admitted the sun into the calendar of the week; and you have selected its day [Sunday], in preference to the preceding day, as the most suitable in the week for either an entire abstinence from the bath, or for its postponement until the evening, or for taking rest, and for banqueting. By resorting to these customs, you deliberately deviate from your own religious rites to those of strangers. For the Jewish feasts are the Sabbath and 'the Purification,' and Jewish also are the ceremonies of the lamps, and the fasts of unleavened bread, and the 'littoral prayers,' all which institutions and practices are of course foreign from your gods. Wherefore, that I may return from this digression, you who reproach us with the sun and Sunday should consider your proximity to us. We are not far off from your Saturn and your days of rest."—*Ad Nationes*, b. i. chap. xiii.

Tertullian in this discourse addresses himself to the nations still in idolatry. The heathen festival of Sunday, which was with some nations more ancient, had been established among the Romans at a comparatively recent date, though earlier than the time of Justin Martyr, the first Christian writer in whom an authentic mention of the day is found. The heathen reproached the early Sunday Christians with being sun-worshipers, "because," says Tertullian, "we pray towards the east, or because we make Sunday a day of festivity." And how does Tertullian answer this grave charge? He could not say, We do it by command of God to honor the first day of the week, for he expressly states in a former quotation that no such precept exists. So he retorts thus: "What then? Do you [heathen] do less than this?" And he adds: "You have selected its day [Sunday] in preference to the preceding day" (Saturday), etc. That is to say, Tertullian wishes to know why, if the heathen could choose Sunday in preference to Saturday, the Christians could not have the same privilege! Could there be a stronger incidental evidence that Sunday was cherished by the early apostatizing Christians, not because commanded of God, but because it was generally observed by their heathen neighbors, and therefore more convenient to them?

But Tertullian next avows his faith in the ten commandments as "the rules of our regenerate life," that is to say, the rules which govern Christian men; and he gives the preference to the seventh day over the eighth:—

> "I must also say something about the period of the soul's birth, that I may omit nothing incidental in the whole process.

> A mature and regular birth takes place, as a general rule, at the commencement of the tenth month. They who theorize respecting numbers, honor the number ten as the parent of all the others, and as imparting perfection to the human nativity. For my own part, I prefer viewing this measure of time in reference to God, as if implying that the ten months rather initiated man into the ten commandments; so that the numerical estimate of the time needed to consummate our natural birth should correspond to the numerical classification of *the rules of our regenerate life*. But inasmuch as birth is also completed with the seventh month, I more readily recognize in this number than in the eighth the honor of a numerical agreement with the Sabbatical period; so that the month in which God's image is sometimes produced in a human birth, shall in its number tally with the day on which God's creation was completed and hallowed." —*De Anima*, chap. xxxvii.

This kind of reasoning is of course destitute of any force. But in adducing such an argument Tertullian avows his faith in the ten commandments as the rule of the Christian's life, gives the preference to the seventh day as the Sabbath, and deduces the origin of the Sabbath from God's act of hallowing the seventh day at creation.

Though Tertullian elsewhere, as we shall see, speaks lightly of the law of God, and represents it as abolished, his next testimony most sacredly honors that law, and while acknowledging the Sabbath as one of its precepts, he recognizes the authority of the whole code. Thus he says:—

> "Of how deep guilt, then, adultery—which is likewise a matter of fornication, in accordance with its criminal function—is to be accounted, the law of God first comes to hand to show us; if it is true [as it is], that after interdicting the superstitious service of alien gods, and the making of idols themselves, after commending [to religious observance] the veneration of the Sabbath, after commanding a religious regard toward parents, second [only to that] toward God, [that law] laid, as the next substratum in strengthening and fortifying such counts, no other precept than 'Thou shalt not commit adultery.'" —*On Modesty*, chap. v.

And of this precept Tertullian presently tells us that it stands "in the very forefront of *the most holy law*, among the primary counts of *the celestial edict*."

In his treatise "On Fasting," chapter xiv., he terms "the Sabbath—a day never to be kept as a fast except at the passover season, according to a reason elsewhere given." And in chapter xv., he excepts from the two weeks in which meat was not eaten "the Sabbaths" and "the Lord's days."

But in his "Answer to the Jews," chapter ii., he represents the law as variously modified from Adam to Christ; he denies "that the Sabbath is still to be observed;" classes it with circumcision; declares that Adam was "inobservant of the Sabbath," affirms the same of Abel, Noah, Enoch, and Melchizedek, and asserts that Lot "was freed from the conflagration of the Sodomites" "for the merits of righteousness, without observance of the law." And in the beginning of chapter iii., he again classes the Sabbath with circumcision, and asserts that Abraham did not "observe the Sabbath."

In chapter iv., he declares that "the observance of the Sabbath" was "temporary." And he continues thus:—

> "For the Jews say, that from the beginning God sanctified the seventh day, by resting on it from all his works which he made; and that thence it was, likewise, that Moses said to the people: 'Remember the day of the Sabbaths,'" etc.

Now see how Tertullian and his brethren disposed of this commandment respecting the seventh day:—

> "Whence we [Christians] understand that *we* still more ought to observe a Sabbath from all 'servile work' always, and not only every seventh day, but through all time."

That is to say in plain language, they would, under pretense of keeping every day as a Sabbath, not only work on the seventh day of the week, but on all the days of the week. But this plainly proves that Tertullian did not think the seventh day was superseded by the first. And thus he proceeds:—

> "And through this arises the question for us, *what* Sabbath God willed us to keep."

Our first-day friends quote Tertullian in behalf of what they call the Christian Sabbath. Had he believed in such an institution he would certainly have named it in answer to this question. But mark his answer:—

> "For the Scriptures point to a Sabbath eternal and a Sabbath temporal. For Isaiah the prophet says, '*Your* Sabbaths my soul hateth.' And in another place he says, 'My Sabbaths ye have profaned.' Whence we discern that the temporal Sabbath is human, and the eternal Sabbath is accounted divine."

This temporal Sabbath is the seventh day; this eternal Sabbath is the keeping of all days alike, as Tertullian affirms that he and those with him did.

He next declares that Isaiah's prediction respecting the Sabbath in the new earth (Isa. 66: 22, 23), was "fulfilled in the times of Christ, when all flesh—that is, every nation—came to adore in Jerusalem God the Father." And he adds: "Thus, therefore, before this temporal Sabbath [the seventh day], there was withal an eternal Sabbath foreshown and foretold," *i. e.*, the keeping of all days alike. And this he fortifies by the assertion that the holy men before Moses did not observe the seventh day. And in proof that the Sabbath was one day to cease, he cites the compassing of Jericho for seven days, one of which must have been the Sabbath. And to this he adds the case of the Maccabees who fought certain battles on the Sabbath. In due time we shall see how admirably he answers such objections as these of his own raising.

In chapter vi., he repeats his theory of the "Sabbath temporal" [the seventh day], and the "Sabbath eternal" or the "Spiritual Sabbath," which is "to observe a Sabbath from all 'servile works' always, and not only every seventh day, but through all time." He says that the ancient law has ceased, and that "the new law" and the "Spiritual Sabbath" have come.

In the twentieth chapter of his first book against Marcion, Tertullian cites Hosea 2:11, and Isa. 1:13, 14, to prove that the Sabbath is now abrogated. And in his fifth book against Marcion, chapter iv., he quotes Gal. 4:10; John 19:31; Isa. 1:13, 14; Amos 5:21, and Hosea 2:11, to prove that "the Creator abolished his own laws," and that he "destroyed the institutions which he set up himself." These quotations are apparently designed to prove that the Sabbath is abolished, but he does not enter into argument from them. But in the nineteenth chapter of this book he quotes Col. 2:16, 17, and simply says of the law: "The apostle here teaches clearly how it has been abolished, even by passing from shadow to substance—that is, from figurative types to the reality, which is Christ." This remark is truthful and would justly exclude the moral law from this abolition.

But in chapter xxi. of his second book against Marcion, he answers the very objection against the Sabbath which himself has elsewhere urged, as we have noticed, drawn from the case of Jericho. He says to Marcion:—

> "You do not, however, consider the law of the Sabbath: they are human works, not divine, which it prohibits. For it says, 'Six days shalt thou labor, and do all thy work; but the seventh day is the Sabbath of the Lord thy God: in it thou shalt not do any work.' What work? Of course your own. The conclusion is, that from the Sabbath day he removes those works which he had before enjoined for the six days, that is, your own works; in other words, human works of daily life. Now, the carrying around of the ark is evidently not an ordinary daily duty, nor yet a human one; but a rare and a sacred work, and, as being then ordered by the direct precept of God, a divine one.... Thus, in the present instance, there is a clear distinction respecting the Sabbath's prohibition of human labors, not divine ones. Accordingly, the man who went and gathered sticks on the Sabbath day was punished with death. For it was his own work which he did; and this the law forbade. They, however, who on the Sabbath carried the ark round Jericho, did it with impunity. For it was not their own work, but God's, which they executed, and that, too, from his express commandment."

In the following chapter he again cites Isa. 1:11-14, as proof that the Sabbath is abolished. He will, however, presently explain this text which he has so many times used against the Sabbath, and show that it actually has no such bearing. In the meantime he will again declare that Joshua did not break the Sabbath, and having done this he will find it in order again to assert that "the Sabbath was actually then broken by Joshua." In his fourth book against Marcion, chapter xii., he discusses the question whether Christ as Lord of the Sabbath had the right to annul the Sabbath, and whether in his life he did actually violate it. To do this he again cites the case of Jericho, and actually affirms that the Sabbath was broken on that occasion, and at the same time denies it. Thus he says:—

> "If Christ interfered with the Sabbath, he simply acted after the Creator's example; inasmuch as in the siege of the city of Jericho the carrying around the walls of the ark of the covenant for eight days running, and therefore on a Sabbath day, actually annulled the Sabbath, by the Creator's command—according to the opinion of those who think this of Christ [Luke 6:1-5] in their ignorance that neither Christ nor the Creator violated the Sabbath, as we shall by-and-by show. And yet the Sabbath was actually then broken by Joshua, so that the present charge might be alleged also against Christ."

The Sabbath was not violated in the case of Jericho, and yet it certainly was there violated! Tertullian adds that if Christ hated the Sabbath he was in this like the Creator himself, who declares [Isa. 1:14] that he hates it. He forgets that the Creator has expressly declared his great regard for the Sabbath by this very prophet [chap. 58:13, 14], and overlooks the fact that what God hates is the hypocritical conduct of the people as set forth in Isaiah 1. In his fourth book against Marcion, chapter xvi., Christ is mentioned as the Lord of the Sabbath, but nothing is said bearing upon Sabbatic obligation. In chapter xxx., of this same book, he alludes to the cure wrought by Christ upon the Sabbath day, mentioned in Luke 13:11-16, and says, "When, therefore, he did a work according to the condition prescribed by the law, he affirmed, instead of breaking, the law," etc.

In the twelfth chapter of this book, however, he asserts many things relative to Christ. He says that the disciples in rubbing out the ears of corn on the Sabbath "had violated the holy day. Christ excuses them and became their accomplice in breaking the Sabbath." He argues that as the Sabbath from the beginning, which he here places at the fall of the manna though elsewhere dating it from the creation, had never been designed as a day of fasting, the Saviour did right in justifying the act of the disciples in the cornfield. And he terms the example of David a "colorable precedent" to justify the eating of the corn. But though he represents the Saviour as "annulling the Sabbath" at this time, he also asserts that in this very case "he maintains the honor of the Sabbath as a day which is to be free from gloom rather than from work." He justifies the Saviour in his acts of healing on the Sabbath, declaring that in this he was doing that which the Sabbath law did not forbid. Tertullian next affirms precisely the reverse of many things which he has advanced against the Sabbath, and even answers his own objections against it. Thus he says:—

> "In order that he might, whilst allowing that amount of work which he was about to perform for a soul, remind them what works the law of the Sabbath forbade—even human works; and what it enjoined—even divine works, which might be done for the benefit of any soul, he was called 'Lord of the Sabbath' because he maintained the Sabbath as his own institution. Now, even if he had annulled the Sabbath, he would have had the right

to do so, as being its Lord, [and] still more as he who instituted it. But lie did not utterly destroy it, although its Lord, in order that it might henceforth be plain that the Sabbath was not broken by the Creator, even at the time when the ark was carried around Jericho. For that was really God's work, which he commanded himself, and which he had ordered for the sake of the lives of his servants when exposed to the perils of war." Book iv. chap. xii.

In this paragraph Tertullian explains the law of God in the clearest manner. He shows beyond all dispute that neither Joshua nor Christ ever violated it. He also declares that Christ did not abolish the Sabbath. In the next sentence he goes on to answer most admirably his own repeated perversion of Isaiah 1:13, 14, and to contradict some of his own serious errors. Listen to him: —

> "Now, although he has in a certain place expressed an aversion of Sabbaths, by calling them '*your Sabbaths*,' reckoning them as men's Sabbaths, not his own, because they were celebrated without the fear of God by a people full of iniquities, and loving God 'with the lip, not the heart,' he has yet put his own Sabbaths (those, that is, which were kept according to his prescription) in a different position; for by the same prophet, in a later passage, he declares them to be 'true, delightful, and inviolable.' [Isa 58:13; 56:2.] Thus *Christ did not at all rescind the Sabbath*: he kept the law thereof, and both in the former case did a work which was beneficial to the life of his disciples (for he indulged them with the relief of food when they were hungry), and in the present instance cured the withered hand; in each case intimating by facts, 'I came not to destroy the law, but to fulfill it,' although Marcion has gagged his mouth by this word."

Here Tertullian shows that God did not hate his own Sabbath, but only the hypocrisy of those who professed to keep it. He also expressly declares that the Saviour "did not at all rescind the Sabbath." And now that he has his hand in, he will not cease till he has testified to a noble Sabbatarian confession of faith, placing its origin at creation, and perpetuating the institution with divine safeguards and additional sanctity. Moreover he asserts that Christ's adversary [Satan] would have had him do this to some other days, a heavy blow as it happens upon those who in modern times so stoutly maintain that he consecrated the first day of the week to take the place of the Creator's rest-day. Listen again to Tertullian, who continues as follows: —

> "For even in the case before us he fulfilled the law, while interpreting its condition; [moreover,] he exhibits in a clear light the different kinds of work, while doing what the law excepts from the sacredness of the Sabbath, [and] while imparting to the Sabbath day itself, which *from the beginning* had been consecrated by the benediction of the Father, an additional sanctity by his own beneficent action. For he furnished to this day divine safeguards, —a course which his adversary would have pursued for some oth-

er days, to avoid honoring the Creator's Sabbath, and restoring to the Sabbath the works which were proper for it. Since, in like manner, the prophet Elisha on this day restored to life the dead son of the Shunammite woman, you see, O Pharisee, and you too, O Marcion, how that it was [proper employment] for the Creator's Sabbaths of old to do good, to save life, not to destroy it; how that Christ introduced nothing new, which was not after the example, the gentleness, the mercy, and the prediction also of the Creator. For in this very example he fulfills the prophetic announcement of a specific healing: 'The weak hands are strengthened,' as were also 'the feeble knees' in the sick of the palsy." —*Tertullian against Marcion*, b. iv. chap. xii.

Tertullian mistakes in his reference to the Shunammite woman. It was not the Sabbath day on which she went to the prophet. 2 Kings 4:23. But in the last three paragraphs quoted from him, which in his work form one continuous statement, he affirms many important truths which are worthy of careful enumeration. They are as follows:—

1. Christ, in determining what should, and what should not, be done on the Sabbath, "was called 'Lord of the Sabbath,' because he maintained the Sabbath as his own institution."

2. "The Sabbath was not broken by the Creator, even at the time when the ark was carried around Jericho."

3. The reason why God expressed his aversion to "your Sabbaths," as though they were "men's Sabbaths, not his own," was "because they were celebrated without the fear of God, by a people full of iniquities." See Isa. 1:13, 14.

4. "By the same prophet [Isa. 58:13; 56:2], he declares them [the Sabbaths] to be 'true and delightful and inviolable.'"

5. "Thus Christ did not at all rescind the Sabbath."

6. "He kept the law thereof."

7. "The Sabbath day itself, which from the beginning had been consecrated by the benediction of the Father." This language expressly assigns the origin of the Sabbath to the act of the Creator at the close of the first week of time.

8. Christ imparted to the Sabbath "an additional sanctity by his own beneficent action."

9. "He furnished to this day divine safeguards,—a course which his adversary would have pursued for some other days, to avoid honoring the Creator's Sabbath, and restoring to the Sabbath the works which were proper for it."

This last statement is indeed very remarkable. Christ furnished "the Creator's Sabbath," the seventh day, with "divine safeguards." His adversary (THE adversary of Christ is the devil) would have had this course "pursued for some other days." That is to say, the devil would have been pleased had Christ consecrated some other day, instead of adding to the sanctity of his Father's Sabbath. What

Tertullian says that the devil would have been pleased to have Christ do, that our first-day friends now assert that he did do in the establishment of what they call the Christian Sabbath! Such an institution, however, was never heard of in the days of the so-called Christian fathers. Notwithstanding Tertullian's many erroneous statements concerning the Sabbath and the law, he has here borne a noble testimony to the truth, and this completes his words.

CHAPTER VIII.

Fabian—Origen—Hippolytus—Novatian.

TESTIMONY OF THE EPISTLES AND DECREES
OF POPE FABIAN.

THIS man was bishop of Rome from A. D. 236 to A. D. 250. The letters ascribed to Fabian were probably written at a considerably later date. We quote them, however, at the very point of time wherein they claim to have been written. Their testimony is of little importance, but they breathe the self-important spirit of a Roman bishop. We quote as follows:—

> "You ought to know what is being done in things sacred in the church of Rome, in order that, by following her example, ye may be found to be true children of her who is called your mother. Accordingly, as we have received the institution from our fathers, we maintain seven deacons in the city of Rome, distributed over seven districts of the state, who attend to the services enjoined on them week by week, and on the Lord's days, and the solemn festivals," etc.—*Epistle First.*

This pope is said to have made the following decree, which contains the only other reference to the so-called Lord's day to be found in the writings attributed to him:—

> "We decree that on each Lord's day the oblation of the altar should be made by all men and women in bread and wine, in order that by means of these sacrifices they may be released from the burden of their sins."—*Decrees of Fabian*, b. v. chap. vii.

In these quotations we see that the Roman church is made the mother of all churches, and also that the Roman bishop thinks himself the rightful ruler over all Christian people. And it is in fit keeping with these features of the great apostasy that the pope, instead of pointing sinful men to the sacrifice made on Calvary, should "decree that on each Lord's day" every person should offer an "oblation" of "bread and wine" on the altar, "that by means of THESE SACRIFICES they may be released from the burden of their sins"!

TESTIMONY OF ORIGEN.

Origen was born about A. D. 185, probably at Alexandria in Egypt. He was a man of immense learning, but unfortunately adopted a spiritualizing system in the interpretation of the Scriptures that was the means of flooding the church with many errors. He wrote during the first half of the third century. I have carefully examined all the writings of every Christian writer preceding the council of Nice with the single exception of Origen. Some of his works, as yet, I have not been able to obtain. While, therefore, I give the entire testimony of every other father on the subject of inquiry, in his case I am unable to do this. But I can give it with sufficient fullness to present him in a just light. His first reference to the Sabbath is a denial that it should be literally understood. Thus he says:—

> "There are countless multitudes of believers who, although unable to unfold methodically and clearly the results of their spiritual understanding, are nevertheless most firmly persuaded that neither ought circumcision to be understood literally, nor the rest of the Sabbath, nor the pouring out of the blood of an animal, nor that answers were given by God to Moses on these points. And this method of apprehension is undoubtedly suggested to the minds of all by the power of the Holy Spirit." —*De Principiis*, b. ii. chap. vii.

Origen asserts that the spiritual interpretation of the Scriptures whereby their literal meaning is set aside is something divinely inspired! But when this is accepted as the truth who can tell what they mean by what they say?

In the next chapter he quotes Isa. 1:13, 14, but with reference to the subject of the soul and not to that of the Sabbath. In chapter xi., alluding again to the hidden meaning of the things commanded in the Scriptures, he asserts that when the Christian has "returned to Christ" he will, amongst other things enumerated, "see also the reasons for the festival days, and holy days, and for all the sacrifices and purifications." So it seems that Origen thought the spiritual meaning of the Sabbath, which he asserted in the place of the literal, was to be known only in the future state!

In book iv. chapter i., he quotes Col. 2:16, but gives no exposition of its meaning. But having asserted that the things commanded in the law were not to be understood literally, and having intimated that their hidden meaning cannot be known until the saints are with Christ, he proceeds in section 17 of this chapter to prove that the literal sense of the law is impossible. One of the arguments by which he proves the point is, that men were commanded not to go out of their houses on the Sabbath. He thus quotes and comments on Ex. 16:29:—

> "'Ye shall sit, every one in your dwellings; no one shall move from his place on the Sabbath day,' which precept it is impossible to observe literally; for no man can sit a whole day so as not to move from the place where he sat down." Origen quotes a certain Samaritan who declares that one must not change his posture on the Sabbath, and he adds, "Moreover the injunction which runs, 'Bear no burden on the Sabbath day,' seems to me an impossibility."

This argument is framed for the purpose of proving that the Scriptures cannot be taken in their literal sense. But had he quoted the text correctly there would be no force at all to his argument. They must not go out to gather manna, but were expressly commanded to use the Sabbath for holy convocations, that is, for religious assemblies. Lev. 23:3. And as to the burdens mentioned in Jer. 17:21-27, they are sufficiently explained by Neh. 13:15-22. Such reasons as these for denying the obvious, simple signification of what God has commanded, are worthy of no confidence. In his letter to Africanus, Origen thus alludes to the Sabbath, but without further remarking upon it:—

> "You will find the law about not bearing a burden on the Sabbath day in Jeremiah as well as in Moses."

Though these allusions of Origen to the Sabbath are not in themselves of much importance, we give them all, that his testimony may be presented as fully as possible. His next mention of the Sabbath seems from the connection to relate to Paul:—

> "Was it impious to abstain from corporeal circumcision, and from a literal Sabbath, and literal festivals, and literal new moons, and from clean and unclean meats, and to turn the mind to the good and true and spiritual law of God," etc.—*Origen against Celsus*, b. ii. chap. vii.

We shall soon get his idea of the true Sabbath as distinguished from the "literal" one. He gives the following reason for the "literal Sabbath" among the Hebrews:—

> "In order that there might be leisure to listen to their sacred laws, the days termed 'Sabbath,' and the other festivals which existed among them, were instituted." Book iv. chap. xxxi.

What Origen mentions as the reason for the institution of the Sabbath is in fact only one of its incidental benefits. The real reason for its institution, viz., that the creation of the heavens and the earth should be remembered, he seems to have overlooked because so literally expressed in the commandment. Of God's rest-day he thus speaks:—

> "With respect, however, to the creation of the world, and the 'rest [*Sabbatismou*] which is reserved after it for the people of God,' the subject is extensive, and mystical, and profound, and difficult of explanation." Book v. chap. lix.

Origen's next mention of the Sabbath not only places the institution of the Sabbath at the creation, but gives us some idea of his "mystical" Sabbath as distinguished from "a literal" one. Speaking of the Creator's rest from the six days' work he thus alludes to Celsus:—

> "For he [Celsus] knows nothing of the day of the Sabbath and rest of God, *which follows the completion of the world's creation*, and *which lasts during the duration of the world*, and in which all those will keep festival with God who have done all *their* works in *their* six days, and who, because they have omitted none of their duties,

will ascend to the contemplation [of celestial things], and to the assembly of righteous and blessed beings." Book vi. chap. lxi.

Here we get an insight into Origen's mystical Sabbath. It began at creation, and will continue while the world endures. To those who follow the letter it is indeed only a weekly rest, but to those who know the truth it is a perpetual Sabbath, enjoyed by God during all the days of time, and entered by believers either at conversion or at death. And this last thought perhaps explains why he said before that the reasons for days observed by the Hebrews would be understood after this life.

But last of all we come to a mention of the so-called Lord's day by Origen. As he has a mystical or perpetual Sabbath like some of the earlier fathers, in which, under pretense of keeping every day as a Sabbath, they actually labor on every one, so has he also, like what we have found in some of them, a Lord's day which is not merely one definite day of the week, but which embraces every day, and covers all time. Here are his words:—

> "For 'to keep a feast,' as one of the wise men of Greece has well said, 'is nothing else than to do one's duty;' and that man truly celebrates a feast who does his duty and prays always, offering up continually bloodless sacrifices in prayer to God. That therefore seems to me a most noble saying of Paul, 'Ye observe days, and months, and times, and years. I am afraid of you, lest I have bestowed upon you labor in vain.'

> "If it be objected to us on this subject that we ourselves are accustomed to observe certain days, as, for example, the Lord's day, the Preparation, the Passover, or Pentecost, I have to answer, that to the perfect Christian, who is ever in his thoughts, words, and deeds, serving his natural Lord, God the Word, *all his days are the Lord's*, and *he is always keeping the Lord's day*." Book viii., close of chapter xxi. and beginning of chapter xxii.

With respect to what he calls the Lord's day, Origen divides his brethren into two classes, as he had before divided the people of God into two classes with respect to the Sabbath. One class are the imperfect Christians, who content themselves with the literal day; the other are the perfect Christians, whose Lord's day embraces all the days of their life. Undoubtedly Origen reckoned himself one of the perfect Christians. His observance of the Lord's day did not consist in the elevation of one day above another, for he counted them all alike as constituting one perpetual Lord's day, the very doctrine which we found in Clement of Alexandria, who was Origen's teacher in his early life. The keeping of the Lord's day with Origen as with Clement embraced all the days of his life, and consisted according to Origen in serving God in thought, word, and deed, continually; or as expressed by Clement, one "keeps the Lord's day when he abandons an evil disposition, and assumes that of the Gnostic."

These things prove that Origen did not count Sunday as the Lord's day to be honored above the other days as a divine memorial of the resurrection, for he kept the Lord's day during every day in the week. Nor did he hold Sunday as the

Lord's day to be kept as a day of abstinence from labor, while all the other days were days of business, for whatever was necessary to keeping Lord's day he did on every day of the week.

As to the imperfect Christians who honored a literal day as the Lord's day, Origen shows what rank it stood in by associating it with the Preparation, the Passover, and the Pentecost, all of which in this dispensation are mere church institutions, and none of them days of abstinence from labor. The change of the Sabbath from the seventh day to the first, or the existence of the so-called Christian Sabbath was in Origen's time absolutely unknown.

TESTIMONY OF HIPPOLYTUS, BISHOP OF PORTUS.

Hippolytus, who was bishop of Portus, near Rome, wrote about A. D. 230. It is evident from his testimony that he believed the Sabbath was made by God's act of sanctifying the seventh day at the beginning. He held that day to be the type of the seventh period of a thousand years. Thus he says:—

> "And 6000 years must needs be accomplished, in order that the Sabbath may come, the rest, the holy day on which God rested from all his works. For the Sabbath is the type and emblem of the future kingdom of the saints, when they shall reign with Christ, when he comes from Heaven, as John says in his Apocalypse: for a day with the Lord is as a thousand years. Since, then, in six days God made all things, it follows that six thousand years must be fulfilled."—*Commentaries on Various Books of Scripture.* Sect. 4, on Daniel.

The churches of Ethiopia have a series of Canons, or church rules, which they attribute to this father. Number thirty-three reads thus:—

> "That commemoration should be made of the faithful dead every day, with the exception of the Lord's day."

The church of Alexandria have also a series which they ascribe to him. The thirty-third is thus given:—

> "Of the *Atalmsas* (the oblation), which they shall present for those who are dead, that it be not done on the Lord's day."

The thirty-eighth one has these words:—

> "Of the night on which our Lord Jesus Christ rose. That no one shall sleep on that night, and wash himself with water."

These are the only things in Hippolytus that can be referred to the Sunday festival. Prayers and offerings for the dead, which we find some fifty years earlier in Tertullian, are, according to Hippolytus, lawful on every day but the so-called Lord's day. They grew up with the Sunday festival, and are of equal authority with it. Tertullian, as we have already observed, tells us frankly that there is no scriptural authority for the one or the other, and that they rest on custom and tradition alone.

TESTIMONY OF NOVATIAN, A ROMAN PRESBYTER.

Novatian, who wrote about A. D. 250, is accounted the founder of the sect called *Cathari*, or *Puritans*. He tried to resist some of the gross corruptions of the church of Rome. He wrote a treatise on the Sabbath, which is not extant. There is no reference to Sunday in any of his writings. In his treatise "On the Jewish Meats," he speaks of the Sabbath thus:—

> "But how perverse are the Jews, and remote from the understanding of their law, I have fully shown, as I believe, in two former letters, wherein it was absolutely proved that they are ignorant of what is the true circumcision, and what the true Sabbath." Chapter i.

If we contrast the doctrine of the Pharisees concerning the Sabbath with the teaching of the Saviour, or with that of Isaiah in his fifty-eighth chapter, we shall not think Novatian far from the truth in his views of the Jewish people. In his treatise "Concerning the Trinity" is the following allusion to the Sabbath:—

> "For in the manner that as man he is of Abraham, so also as God he is before Abraham himself. And in the same manner as he is as man the 'Son of David,' so as God he is proclaimed David's Lord. And in the same manner as he was made as man 'under the law,' so as God he is declared to be 'Lord of the Sabbath.'" Chapter xi.

These are the only references to the Sabbath in what remains of the writings of Novatian. He makes the following striking remarks concerning the moral law:—

> "The law was given to the children of Israel for this purpose, that they might profit by it, and RETURN *to those virtuous manners*, which, although *they have received them from their fathers*, they had corrupted in Egypt by reason of their intercourse with a barbarous people. Finally, also, those *ten commandments* on the tables *teach nothing new*, but *remind* them of *what had been obliterated*— that righteousness in them, which had been put to sleep, might revive again as it were by the afflatus of the law, after the manner of a fire [nearly extinguished]." —*On the Jewish Meats*, chap. iii.

It is therefore certain that in the judgment of Novatian, the ten commandments enjoined nothing that was not sacredly regarded by the patriarchs before that Jacob went down into Egypt. It follows, therefore, that in his opinion the Sabbath was made, not at the fall of the manna, but when God sanctified the seventh day, and that holy men from the earliest ages observed it. The Sunday festival with its varied names and titles he never mentions.

CHAPTER IX.

Cyprian—Dionysius of Alexandria—Anatolius—Commodianus—
Archelaus.

TESTIMONY OF CYPRIAN, BISHOP OF CARTHAGE.

CYPRIAN wrote about A. D. 255. I find only two references to Sunday in his works. The first is in his thirty-second epistle (the thirty-eighth of the Oxford edition), in which he says of one Aurelius that "he reads on the Lord's day" for him. But in the second instance he defines the meaning of the term, and gives evidence in support of his application of it to the first day of the week. He is arguing in behalf of infant baptism, or rather in controverting the opinion that baptism should be deferred till the child is eight days old. Though the command to circumcise infants when eight days of age is one of the chief grounds of authority for infant baptism, yet the time in that precept according to Cyprian does not indicate the age of the child to be baptized, but prefigures the fact that the eighth day is the Lord's day. Thus he says:—

> "For in respect of the observance of the eighth day in the Jewish circumcision of the flesh, a sacrament was given beforehand in shadow and in usage; but when Christ came, it was fulfilled in truth. For because the eighth day, that is, the first day after the Sabbath, was to be that on which the Lord should rise again, and should quicken us, and give us circumcision of the Spirit, the eighth day, that is, the first day after the Sabbath, and the Lord's day, went before in the figure; which figure ceased when by and by the truth came, and spiritual circumcision was given to us."— *Epistle* lviii. sect. 4; in the Oxford edition, *Epistle* lxiv.

Circumcision is made to prove twin errors of the great apostasy, *infant baptism* and that *the eighth day is the Lord's day*. But the eighth day in the case of circumcision was not the day succeeding the seventh, that is, the first day of the week, but the eighth day of the life of each infant, and therefore it fell on one day of the week as often as upon another. Such is the only argument addressed by Cyprian for first-day sacredness, and this one seems to have been borrowed from Justin Martyr, who, as we have seen, used it about one hundred years before him. It is however quite as weighty as the argument of Clement of Alexandria, who adduced in its support what he calls a prophecy of the eighth day out of the writings of the heathen philosopher Plato! And both are in the same rank with that of Tertullian, who confessed that they had not the authority of Scripture, but accepted in its stead that of custom and tradition!

In his "Exhortation to Martyrdom," section 11, Cyprian quotes the larger part of Matt. 24, and in that quotation at verse 20, the Sabbath is mentioned, but he says nothing concerning that institution. In his "Testimonies against the Jews," book i., sections 9 and 10, he says "that the former law which was given by Moses, was about to cease," and that "a new law was to be given;" and in the conclusion of his "Treatise against the Jews," section 119, he says "that the yoke of the law was heavy which is cast off by us," but it is not certain that he meant to include in these statements the precepts of the moral law.

TESTIMONY OF DIONYSIUS, BISHOP OF ALEXANDRIA.

This father, who was one of Origen's disciples, wrote about A. D. 260. In the first canon of his "Epistle to Bishop Basilides" he treats of "the proper hour for bringing the fast to a close on the day of Pentecost." He has occasion to quote what the four evangelists say of the Sabbath and first-day in connection with the resurrection of Christ. But in doing this he adds not one word expressive of first-day sacredness, nor does he give it any other title than that of plain "first day of the week." The seventh day is simply called "the Sabbath." He also speaks of "the preparation and the Sabbath" as the "last two days" of a six days' fast, at the anniversary of the week of Christ's death.

TESTIMONY OF ANATOLIUS, BISHOP OF LAODICEA.

This father wrote about A. D. 270. He participated in the discussion of the question whether the festival of Easter, or passover, should be celebrated on the fourteenth day of the first month, the same day on which the Jews observed the passover, or whether it should be observed on the so-called Lord's day next following. In this discussion he uses the term Lord's day, in his first canon once, quoting it from Origen; in his seventh, twice; in his tenth, twice; in his eleventh, four times; in his twelfth, once; in his sixteenth, twice. These are all the instances in which he uses the term. We quote such of them as shed any light upon the meaning of it as used by him. In his seventh canon he says: "The obligation of the Lord's resurrection binds to keep the paschal festival on the Lord's day." In his tenth canon he uses this language: "The solemn festival of the resurrection of the Lord can be celebrated only on the Lord's day." And also "that it should not be lawful to celebrate the Lord's mystery of the passover at any other time but on the Lord's day, on which the resurrection of the Lord from death took place, and on which rose also for us the cause of everlasting joy." In his eleventh canon he says: "On the Lord's day was it that light was shown to us in the beginning, and now also in the end, the comforts of all present and the tokens of all future blessings." In his sixteenth canon he says: "Our regard for the Lord's resurrection which took place on the Lord's day will lead us to celebrate it on the same principle."

The reader may be curious to know why a controversy should have arisen respecting the proper day for the celebration of the passover in the Christian church when no such celebration had ever been commanded. The explanation is this: The festival was celebrated solely on the authority of tradition, and there were in this case two directly conflicting traditions, as is fully shown in the tenth canon of this father. One party had their tradition from John the apostle, and held that the paschal feast should be celebrated every year "whenever the fourteenth day of the moon had come, and the lamb was sacrificed by the Jews." But the other party had their tradition from the apostles Peter and Paul that this festival should not be celebrated on that day, but upon the so-called Lord's day next following. And so a fierce controversy arose which was decided in A. D. 325, by the council of Nice, in favor of Saint Peter, who had on his side his pretended successor, the powerful and crafty bishop of Rome.

The term Lord's day is never applied to Sunday till the closing years of the second century. And Clement, who is the first to make such an application, represents the true Lord's day as made up of every day of the Christian's life. And this opinion is avowed by others after him.

But after we enter the third century the name Lord's day is quite frequently applied to Sunday. Tertullian, who lived at the epoch where we first find this application, frankly declares that the festival of Sunday, to which he gives the name of Lord's day, had no Scriptural authority, but that it was founded upon tradition. But should not the traditions of the third century be esteemed sufficient authority for calling Sunday the Lord's day? The very men of that century who speak thus of Sunday strenuously urge the observance of the feast of the passover. Shall we accept this festival which they offer to us on the authority of their apostolic tradition? As if to teach us the folly of adding tradition to the Bible as a part of our rule of faith, it happens that there are, even from the early part of the second century, two directly conflicting traditions as to what day should be kept for the passover. And one party had theirs from Saint John, the other had theirs from Saint Peter and Saint Paul! And it is very remarkable that although each of these parties claimed to know from one or the other of these apostles that they had the right day for the passover and the other had the wrong one, there is never a claim by one of these fathers that Sunday is the Lord's day because John on the isle of Patmos called it such! If men in the second and third centuries were totally mistaken in their traditions respecting the passover, as they certainly were, shall we consider the traditions of the third century sufficient authority for asserting that the title of Lord's day belongs to Sunday by apostolic authority?

TESTIMONY OF COMMODIANUS.

This person was a native of Africa, and does not appear to have ever held any office in the Christian church. He wrote about A. D. 270. The only allusions made by him to the Sabbath are in the following words addressed to the Jews:—

"There is not an unbelieving people such as yours. O evil men! in so many places, and so often rebuked by the law of those who cry aloud. And the Lofty One despises your Sabbaths, and altogether rejects your universal monthly feasts according to law, that ye should not make to him the commanded sacrifices; who told you to throw a stone for your offense." —*Instructions in Favor of Christian Discipline*, sect. 40.

This statement is very obscure, and there is nothing in the connection that sheds any light upon it. His language may have reference to the ceremonial sabbaths, or it may include also the Sabbath of the Lord. If it includes the Sabbath made for man it may be intended, like the words of Isa. 1:13, 14, to rebuke the hypocrisy of those who profess to keep it rather than to condemn the institution itself.

He makes only one use of the term Lord's day, and that is as obscure as is his reference to the subject of the Sabbath. Here it is:—

> "Neither dost thou fear the Lord, who cries aloud with such an utterance; even he who commands us to give food even to our enemies. Look forward to thy meals from that Tobias who always on *every day* shared them entirely with the poor man. Thou seekest to feed him, O fool, who feedeth thee again. Dost thou wish that he should prepare for me, who is setting before him his burial? The brother oppressed with want, nearly languishing away, cries out at the splendidly fed, and with distended belly. What sayest thou of the Lord's day? If he have not placed himself before, call forth a poor man from the crowd whom thou mayest take to thy dinner. In the tablets is your hope from a Christ refreshed." Section 61.

Whether Commodianus meant to charge his brethren to relieve the hungry on one day only of the week, or whether he held to such a Lord's day as that of Clement of Alexandria, Origen, and others (namely, one that includes every day of the life of him who refrains from sin), and so would have his brethren imitate Tobias, who fed the hungry *every day*, must be left undetermined. He could not have believed that Sunday was the Lord's day by divine appointment, for he refers to the passover festival (which rests solely upon the traditions and commandments of men) as coming "once in the year" and he designates it as "Easter that day of ours *most blessed*." Section 75. The day of the passover was therefore in his estimation the most sacred day in the Christian church.

TESTIMONY OF ARCHELAUS, BISHOP OF CASCAR.

This person wrote about A. D. 277, or according to other authorities he wrote not far from A. D. 300. He flourished in Mesopotamia. What remains of his writings is simply the record of his "Disputation with Manes," the heretic. I do not find that he ever uses the term "Lord's day." He introduces the Sabbath and states his views of it thus:—

> "Moses, that illustrious servant of God, committed to those who wished to have the right vision, an emblematic law, and also a real law. Thus, to take an example, after God had made the world, and all things that are in it, in the space of six days, he rested on the seventh day from all his works; by which statement I do not mean to affirm that he rested because he was fatigued, but that he did so as having brought to its perfection every creature

which he had resolved to introduce. And yet in the sequel it (the new law) says: 'My Father worketh hitherto, and I work.' Does that mean, then, that he is still making heaven, or sun, or man, or animals, or trees, or any such thing? Nay; but the meaning is, that when these visible objects were perfectly finished, he rested from that kind of work; while, however, he still continues to work at objects invisible with an inward mode of action, and saves men. In like manner, then, the legislator desires also that every individual among us should be devoted unceasingly to this kind of work, even as God himself is; and he enjoins us consequently to rest continuously from secular things, and to engage in no worldly sort of work whatsoever; and this is called our Sabbath. This he also added in the law, that nothing senseless should be done, but that we should be careful and direct our life in accordance with what is just and righteous." Section 31.

These words appear to teach that he held to a perpetual Sabbath, like Justin Martyr, Tertullian, and others. Yet this does not seem possible, inasmuch as, unlike Justin, who despises what he calls days of "idleness," this writer says that we are "to engage in no worldly sort of work whatsoever and this is that our Sabbath." It is hardly possible that he could hold it a wicked thing to labor on one or all of the six working days. Yet he either means to assert that it is sinful to work on a single one of the days, or else he asserts the perpetual obligation of that Sabbath which it is manifest he believed originated when God set apart the seventh day, and which he acknowledges on the authority of what "he also added in the law." We shall shortly come to his final statement, which seems clearly to show that the second of these views was the one held by this writer.

After showing in this same section that the death penalty at the hand of the magistrate for the violation of the Sabbath is no longer in force because of forgiveness through the Saviour, and after answering the objection of Manes in sections 40, 41, 42, that Christ in healing on the Sabbath directly contradicted what Moses did to those who in his time violated the Sabbath, he states his views of the perpetuity of the ancient Sabbath in very clear language. Thus he says:—

"Again, as to the assertion that the Sabbath has been abolished, we deny that he has abolished it plainly (*plane*); for he was himself also Lord of the Sabbath. And this (the law's relation to the Sabbath) was like the servant who has charge of the bridegroom's couch, and who prepares the same with all carefulness, and does not suffer it to be disturbed or touched by any stranger, but keeps it intact against the time of the bridegroom's arrival; so that when he is come, the bed may be used as it pleases himself, or as it is granted to those to use it whom he has bidden enter along with him." Section 42.

Three things are plainly taught. 1. The law sacredly guarded the Sabbath till the coming of Christ. 2. When Christ came, he did not abolish the Sabbath, for he was its Lord. 3. And the whole tenor of this writer's language shows that he had no knowledge of the change of the Sabbath in honor of Christ's resurrection, nor does he even once allude to the first day of the week.

CHAPTER X.

Victorinus—Peter—Methodius—Lactantius—Poem   on   Genesis—
    Conclusion.

TESTIMONY OF VICTORINUS, BISHOP OF PETAU.

THIS person wrote about A. D. 300. His bishopric was in Germany. Of his work
on the "Creation of the World," only a fragment is now preserved. In the first
section he speaks thus of the sanctification of the seventh day:—

> "God produced that entire mass for the adornment of his maj-
> esty in six days; on the seventh to which he consecrated it [some
> words are here lost out of the text] with a blessing. For this reason,
> therefore, because in the septenary number of days both heavenly
> and earthly things are ordered, in place of the beginning. I will
> consider of this seventh day after the principle of all matters per-
> taining to the number seven."

Victorinus, like some other of the fathers, held that the "true and just Sabbath should be observed in the seventh millenary." He believed that the Sabbath
was abolished by the Saviour. He was in sympathy with the act of the church of
Rome in turning the Sabbath into a fast. He held to a two days' weekly fast, as his
words necessarily imply. He would have men fast on the sixth day to commemorate Christ's death, and on the seventh, lest they should seem to keep the Sabbath
with the Jews, but on the so-called Lord's day they were to go forth to their bread
with giving of thanks. Thus he reasons:—

> "On this day [the sixth] also, on account of the passion of the
> Lord Jesus Christ, we make either a station to God, or a fast. On
> the seventh day he rested from all his works, and blessed it, and
> sanctified it. On the former day [the sixth] we are accustomed to
> fast rigorously, that on the Lord's day we may go forth to our
> bread with giving of thanks. And let the *parasceve* [the sixth day]
> become a rigorous fast, lest we should appear to observe any Sab-
> bath with the Jews, which Christ himself, the Lord of the Sabbath,
> says by his prophet that 'his soul hateth;' which Sabbath he in
> his body abolished, although, however, he had formerly himself
> commanded Moses that circumcision should not pass over the
> eighth day, which day very frequently happens on the Sabbath,
> as we read written in the gospel. Moses, foreseeing the hardness
> of that people, on the Sabbath raised up his hands, therefore,

and thus fastened himself to a cross. And in the battle they were sought for by the foreigners on the Sabbath day, that they might be taken captive, and, as if by the very strictness of the law, might be fashioned to the avoidance of its teachings." Section 4.

These statements are in general of little consequence, but some of them deserve notice. First, we have one of the grand elements which contributed to the abandonment of the Sabbath of the Lord, viz., hatred toward the Jews for their conduct toward Christ. Those who acted thus forgot that Christ himself was the Lord of the Sabbath, and that it was his institution and not that of the Jews to which they were doing despite. Secondly, it was the church of Rome that turned the Sabbath into a fast one hundred years before this, in order to suppress its observance, and Victorinus was acting under its instructions. Thirdly, we have a reference to the so-called Lord's day, as a day of thanksgiving, but no connection between it and the Sabbath is indicated for in his time the change of the Sabbath had not been thought of. He has other reasons for neglecting the seventh day which here follow:—

"And thus in the sixth psalm for the eighth day, David asks the Lord that he would not rebuke him in his anger, nor judge him in his fury; for this is indeed the eighth day of that future judgment, which will pass beyond the order of the sevenfold arrangement. Jesus also, the son of Nave, the successor of Moses, himself broke the Sabbath day; for on the Sabbath day he commanded the children of Israel to go round the walls of the city of Jericho with trumpets, and declare war against the aliens. Matthias also, prince of Judah, broke the Sabbath; for he slew the prefect of Antiochus the king of Syria on the Sabbath, and subdued the foreigners by pursuing them. And in Matthew we read, that it is written Isaiah also and the rest of his colleagues broke the Sabbath—that that true and just Sabbath should be observed in the seventh millenary of years. Wherefore to those seven days the Lord attributed to each a thousand years; for thus went the warning: 'In mine eyes, 0 Lord, a thousand years are as one day.' Therefore in the eyes of the Lord each thousand of years is ordained, for I find that the Lord's eyes are seven. Wherefore, as I have narrated, that true Sabbath will be in the seventh millenary of years, when Christ with his elect shall reign." Section 5.

This completes the testimony of Victorinus. He evidently held that the Sabbath originated at the sanctification of the seventh day, but for the reasons here given, the most of which are trivial, and all of which are false, he held that it was abolished by Christ. His argument from the sixth psalm, and from Isaiah's violation of the Sabbath, is something extraordinary. He had an excellent opportunity to say that though the seventh-day Sabbath was abolished, yet we have the Christian Sabbath, or the Lord's day, to take its place. But he shows positively that he knew of no such institution; for he says, "That true and just Sabbath" will be "in the seventh millenary of years."

TESTIMONY OF PETER, BISHOP OF ALEXANDRIA.

This father wrote about A. D. 306. In his "Canon 15" he thus sets forth the celebration of the fourth, the sixth, and the first days of the week:—

> "No one shall find fault with us for observing the fourth day of the week, and the preparation [the sixth day], on which it is reasonably enjoined us to fast according to the tradition. On the fourth day, indeed, because on it the Jews took counsel for the betrayal of the Lord; and on the sixth, because on it he himself suffered for us. But the Lord's day we celebrate as a day of joy, because on it he rose again, on which day we have received it for a custom not even to bow the knee."

On this Balsamon, an ancient writer whose commentary is appended to this canon, remarks that this canon is in harmony with the 64th apostolical canon, which declares "that we are not to fast on the Sabbath, with one exception, the great Sabbath [the one connected with the passover], and to the 69th canon, which severely punishes those who do not fast in the Holy Lent, and on every fourth day of the week and day of preparation." So it appears that they were commanded by the canons to fast on the fourth and sixth days of the week, and forbidden to do this on the Sabbath and first-day.

Zonaras, another ancient commentator upon the canons of Peter, gives us the authority upon which these observances rest. No one of these three days is honored by God's commandment. Zonaras mentions the fasts on the fourth and sixth days, and says no one will find fault with these. But he deems it proper to mark Peter's reason for the Lord's-day festival, and the nature of that festival. Thus he says:—

> "But on the Lord's day we ought not to fast, for it is a day of joy for the resurrection of the Lord, and on it, says he, we have received that we ought not even to bow the knee. This word, therefore, is to be carefully observed, 'we have received' and 'it is enjoined upon us according to the tradition.' For from hence it is evident that long-established custom was taken for law. Moreover, the great Basil annexes also the causes for which it was forbidden to bend the knee on the Lord's day, and from the passover to Pentecost."

The honors which were conferred upon this so-called Lord's day are specified. They are two in number. 1. It was "a day of joy," and therefore not a day of fasting. 2. On it they "ought not even to bow the knee." This last honor however applied to the entire period of fifty days between the passover and the Pentecost as well as to each Sunday in the year. So that the first honor was the only one which belonged to Sunday exclusively. That honor excluded fasting, but it is never said to exclude labor, or to render it sinful. And the authority for these two first-day honors is frankly given. It is not the words of holy Scripture nor the commandment of God, but "it is enjoined upon us according to the tradition. For from hence it is evident that long-established custom was taken for law." Such is the testimony of men who knew the facts. In our days men dare not thus acknowledge them, and therefore they assert that the fourth commandment has been changed by divine authority, and that it is sinful to labor upon the first day of the week.

TESTIMONY OF METHODIUS, BISHOP OF TYRE.

This father wrote about A. D. 308, and suffered martyrdom in A. D. 312. A considerable portion of his writings have come down to our time, but in them all I find not one mention of the first day of the week. He held to the perpetuity of the ten commandments, for he says of the beast with ten horns:—

> "Moreover, the ten horns and stings which he is said to have upon his heads are the ten opposites, O virgins, to the decalogue, by which he was accustomed to gore and cast down the souls of many, imagining and contriving things in opposition to the law, 'Thou shalt love the Lord thy God,' and to the other precepts which follow."—*Banquet of the Ten Virgins*, Discourse viii. chap. xiii.

In commenting on the feast of tabernacles (Lev. 23:39-43) he says:—

> "These things being like air and phantom shadows, foretell the resurrection and the putting up of our tabernacle that had fallen upon the earth, which at length, in the seventh thousand of years, resuming again immortal, we shall celebrate the great feast of true tabernacles in the new and indissoluble creation, the fruits of the earth having been gathered in, and men no longer begetting and begotten, but God resting from the works of creation." Discourse ix. chap. i.

Methodius understood the six days of creation, and the seventh day sanctified by the Creator, to teach that at the end of 6000 years the great day of joy shall come to the saints of God:—

> "For since in six days God made the heaven and the earth, and finished the whole world, and rested on the seventh day from all his works which he had made, and blessed the seventh day and sanctified it, so by a figure in the seventh month, when the fruits of the earth have been gathered in, we are commanded to keep the feast to the Lord, which signifies that, when this world shall be terminated at the seventh thousand years, when God shall have completed the world, he shall rejoice in us." Discourse ix. chap. i. sect. 4.

In the fifth chapter of this discourse he speaks of the day of Judgment as "the millennium of rest, which is called the seventh day, even the true Sabbath." He believed that each day of the first seven represented one thousand years, and so the true Sabbath of the Lord sets forth the final triumph of the saints in the seventh period of a thousand years. And in his work "On Things Created," section 9, he refers to this representation of one day as a thousand years, and quotes in proof of it Ps. 90:2, 4. Then he says:—

> "For when a thousand years are reckoned as one day in the sight of God, and from the creation of the world to his rest is six days, so also to our time, six days are defined, as those say who are clever arithmeticians. Therefore, they say that an age of six thousand years extends from Adam to our time. For they say that the Judgment will come on the seventh day, that is, in the seventh thousand years."

The only weekly Sabbath known to Methodius was the ancient seventh day sanctified by God in Eden. He does not intimate that this divine institution has been abolished; and what he says of the ten commandments implies the reverse of that, and he certainly makes no allusion to the festival of Sunday, which on the authority of "custom" and "tradition" had been by so many elevated above the Sabbath of the Lord.

TESTIMONY OF LACTANTIUS.

Lactantius was born in the latter half of the third century, was converted about A. D. 315, and died at Treves about A. D. 325. He was very eminent as a teacher of rhetoric, and was intrusted with the education of Crispus, the son of Constantine. The writings of Lactantius are quite extensive; they contain, however, no reference to the first day of the week. Of the Sabbath he speaks twice. In the first instance he says that one reason alleged by the Jews for rejecting Christ was,

> "That he destroyed the obligation of the law given by Moses; that is, that he did not rest on the Sabbath, but labored for the good of men," etc.—*Divine Institutes*, b. iv. chap. xvii.

It is not clear whether Lactantius believed that Christ violated the Sabbath, nor whether he did away with the moral law while teaching the abrogation of the ceremonial code. But he bears a most decisive testimony to the origin of the Sabbath at creation:—

> "God completed the world and this admirable work of nature in the space of six days (as is contained in the secrets of holy Scripture), and CONSECRATED the seventh day, on which he had rested from his works. But this is the Sabbath day, which in the language of the Hebrews received its name from the number, whence the seventh is the legitimate and complete number." Book vii. chap. xiv.

It is certain that Lactantius did not regard the Sabbath as the memorial of the flight out of Egypt, but as that of the creation of the heavens and the earth. He also believed that the seven days prefigured the seven thousand years of our earth's history:—

> "Therefore, since all the works of God were completed in six days, the world must continue in its present state through six ages, that is, six thousand years. For the great day of God is limit-

ed by a circle of a thousand years, as the prophet shows, who says, 'In thy sight, O Lord, a thousand years are as one day.' And as God labored during those six days in creating such great works, so his religion and truth must labor during these six thousand years, while wickedness prevails and bears rule. And again, since God, having finished his works, rested the seventh day and blessed it, at the end of the six thousandth year all wickedness must be abolished from the earth, and righteousness reign for a thousand years and there must be tranquility and rest from the labors which the world now has long endured." Book vii. chap. xiv.

Thus much for Lactantius. He could not have believed in first-day sacredness, and there is no clear evidence that he held to the abrogation of the Sabbath. Finally we come to a poem on Genesis by an unknown author, but variously attributed to Cyprian, to Victorinus, to Tertullian, and to later writers.

TESTIMONY OF THE POEM ON GENESIS.

"The seventh came, when God
At his works' end did rest, DECREEING IT
SACRED UNTO THE COMING AGES' JOYS."

Lines 51-53.

Here again we have an explicit testimony to the divine appointment of the seventh day to a holy use while man was yet in Eden, the garden of God. And this completes the testimony of the fathers to the time of Constantine and the Council of Nice.

One thing is everywhere open to the reader's eye as he passes through these testimonies from the fathers: they lived in what may with propriety be called the age of apostatizing. The apostasy was not complete, but it was steadily developing itself. Some of the fathers had the Sabbath in the dust, and honored as their weekly festival the day of the sun, though claiming for it no divine authority. Others recognize the Sabbath as a divine institution which should be honored by all mankind in memory of the creation, and yet at the same time they exalt above it the festival of Sunday, which they acknowledge had nothing but custom and tradition for its support. The end may be foreseen: in due time the Sunday festival obtained the whole ground for itself, and the Sabbath was driven out. Several things conspired to accomplish this result:—

1. The Jews, who retained the ancient Sabbath, had slain Christ. It was easy for men to forget that Christ as Lord of the Sabbath had claimed it as his institution, and to call the Sabbath a Jewish institution which Christians should not regard.

2. The church of Rome as the chief in the work of apostasy took the lead in the earliest effort to suppress the Sabbath by turning it into a fast.

3. In the Christian church almost from the beginning men voluntarily honored the fourth, the sixth, and the first days of the week to commemorate the betrayal, the death, and the resurrection of Christ, acts of respect in themselves innocent

enough.

4. But the first day of the week corresponded to the widely observed heathen festival of the sun, and it was therefore easy to unite the honor of Christ with the convenience and worldly advantage of his people, and to justify the neglect of the ancient Sabbath by stigmatizing it as a Jewish institution with which Christians should have no concern.

The *progressive* character of the work of apostasy with respect to the Sabbath is incidentally illustrated by what Giesler, the distinguished historian of the church, says of the Sabbath and first-day in his record of the first, the second, and the third century. Of the first century he says:—

> "Whilst the Christians of Palestine, who kept the whole Jewish law, celebrated of course all the Jewish festivals, the heathen converts observed only the Sabbath, and, in remembrance of the closing scenes of our Saviour's life, the passover (1 Cor. 5:6-8), though without the Jewish superstitions, Gal. 4:10; Col. 2:16. Besides these the Sunday as the day of our Saviour's resurrection (Acts 20:7; 1 Cor. 16:2; Rev. 1:10), ἡ κυριακὴ ἡμέρα, was devoted to religious worship."—*Giesler's Ecclesiastical History*, vol. i. sect. 29, edition 1836.

Sunday having obtained a foothold, see how the case stands in the second century. Here are the words of Giesler again:—

> "Both Sunday and the Sabbath were observed as festivals; the latter however without the Jewish superstitions therewith connected."—*Id.* vol. i. sect. 52.

This time, as Giesler presents the case, Sunday has begun to get the precedence. But when he gives the events of the third century he drops the Sabbath from his record and gives the whole ground to the Sunday and the yearly festivals of the church. Thus he says:—

> "In Origen's time the Christians had no general festivals, excepting the Sunday, the Parasceve (or preparation), the passover, and the feast of Pentecost. Soon after, however, the Christians in Egypt began to observe the festival of the Epiphany, on the sixth of January."—*Id.* vol. i. sect. 70.

These three statements of Giesler, relating as they do to the first, second, and third centuries, are peculiarly calculated to mark the progress of the work of apostasy. Coleman tersely states this work in these words:—

> "The observance of the Lord's day was ordered while the Sabbath of the Jews was continued; nor was the latter superseded until the former had acquired the same solemnity and importance, which belonged, at first, to that great day which God originally ordained and blessed.... But in time, after the Lord's day was fully established, the observance of the Sabbath of the Jews was gradually discontinued, and was finally denounced as heretical."—*An-*

cient Christianity Exemplified, chap. xxvi. sect. 2.

We have traced the work of apostasy in the church of Christ, and have noted the combination of circumstances which contributed to suppress the Sabbath, and to elevate the first day of the week. And now we conclude this series of testimonies out of the fathers by stating the well-known but remarkable fact, that at the very point to which we are brought by these testimonies, the emperor Constantine while yet, according to Mosheim, a heathen, put forth the following edict, A. D. 321, concerning the ancient Sunday festival:—

> "Let all the judges and town people, and the occupation of all trades, rest on the venerable day of the sun: but let those who are situated in the country, freely and at full liberty, attend to the business of agriculture; because it often happens that no other day is so fit for sowing corn and planting vines; lest, the critical moment being let slip, men should lose the commodities granted by Heaven."

By the act of a wicked man the heathen festival of Sunday has now ascended the throne of the Roman Empire. We cannot here follow its history through the long ages of papal darkness and apostasy. But as we close, we cite the words of Mosheim respecting this law as a positive proof that up to this time, as shown from the fathers, Sunday had been a day of ordinary labor when men were not engaged in worship. He says of it:—

> "The first day of the week, which was the ordinary and stated time for the public assemblies of the Christians, *was, in consequence of a peculiar law enacted by Constantine, observed with greater solemnity than it had formerly been."* —Mosheim, century 4, part ii. chap. iv. sect. 5.

This law restrained merchants and mechanics, but did not hinder the farmer in his work. Yet it caused the day to be observed with greater solemnity than formerly it had been. These words are spoken with reference to Christians, and prove that in Mosheim's judgment, as a historian, Sunday was a day on which ordinary labor was customary and lawful with them prior to A. D. 321, as the record of the fathers indicates, and as many historians testify.

But even after this the Sabbath once more rallied, and became strong even in the so-called Catholic church, until the Council of Laodicea A. D. 364 prohibited its observance under a grievous curse. Thenceforward its history is principally to be traced in the records of those bodies which the Catholic church has anathematized as heretics.

Lector House believes that a society develops through a two-fold approach of continuous learning and adaptation, which is derived from the study of classic literary works spread across the historic timeline of literature records. Therefore, we aim at reviving, repairing and redeveloping all those inaccessible or damaged but historically as well as culturally important literature across subjects so that the future generations may have an opportunity to study and learn from past works to embark upon a journey of creating a better future.

This book is a result of an effort made by Lector House towards making a contribution to the preservation and repair of original ancient works which might hold historical significance to the approach of continuous learning across subjects.

HAPPY READING & LEARNING!

LECTOR HOUSE LLP
E-MAIL: lectorpublishing@gmail.com